Moral Analysis

SUNY Series in Philosophy
Robert Cummings Neville, Editor

Moral Analysis

FOUNDATIONS, GUIDES, AND APPLICATIONS

Louis G. Lombardi

Department of Philosophy
Lake Forest College

State University of New York Press

Published by
State University of New York Press, Albany

For information, address State University of New York
Press, State University Plaza, Albany, NY 12246

Library of Congress Cataloging-in-Publication Data

Lombardi, Louis G., 1952–
      Moral analysis.

      (SUNY series in philosophy)
      Includes index.
      1. Ethics.   I. Title.   II. Series.
BJ1012.L66   1988   170   87-12469
ISBN 0-88706-665-8
ISBN 0-88706-666-6 (pbk.)

Contents

Preface

E very one of us can expect to face significant moral problems,
from whether to register for the draft to how to raise children.
Though the issues are common, people are not naturally equipped to
deal with them. Unfortunately, moral problems do not have any standard format; there are no formulas from which quick solutions can be
derived. This does not mean, however, that there are no fruitful
strategies for dealing with moral dilemmas. This book develops and
applies a framework for thinking about moral issues.

I divide moral analysis into three stages:

1. *Foundations*: analysis of the moral considerations that must be
   used in deliberations;

2. *Action Guides*: the general obligations that result from moral considerations; these include the commonly-accepted rules (like "Do
   not steal!") that people often appeal to as appropriate standards of
   conduct; and

3. *Applications* of Action Guides to Specific Cases or Types of Situations: here arise judgments of how to act when given a particular
   set of circumstances.

There is a natural progression through the book, as these stages are
elaborated. Each chapter is, however, a self-contained discussion of a
particular feature of moral analysis.

Chapters I and II elaborate the foundations of moral analysis. An
examination of human nature uncovers two basic moral considerations: welfare and freedom. These are developed in light of utilitarian

and deontological moral theories, but with an emphasis on points of convergence more than differences. The discussion is designed not to invite a choice as to which theory is best but to highlight the variety of basic values or considerations that routinely enter moral discussions. These considerations are developed and applied throughout the book.

Chapters III and IV move to the second stage of moral analysis: action guides. Different types of moral action guides are described and related to other guides, such as self-interest and law. Chapters V and VI elaborate further issues that arise in the first two stages of moral analysis: (1) whether moral considerations should be extended to animals and other living things, and (2) how the concept of rights functions as a type of action guide.

Chapters VII through IX apply the previously developed framework to specific moral controversies, that is, abortion, whistle blowing, and one relationship between morality and law. Though much work in practical ethics focuses on this stage, little attention has been devoted to providing people with the theoretical framework from which to deal with these complex moral problems. I hope that an understanding of the framework elaborated here will provide the necessary theoretical underpinnings.

In putting this book together, I have benefitted from the encouragement and suggestions of numerous people. My colleague Forest Hansen offered both throughout the process. The first draft was written with the help of a Lake Forest College Summer Research Grant, provided by Dean Bailey Donnally. Comments from Professor G. Donald Hollenhorst, students in numerous applied ethics courses, my colleagues on the Values Education Committee, participants at various professional meetings, and Carola Sautter and the reviewers of SUNY Press were extremely helpful. Finally, I want to thank Dan Brock and B. J. Diggs, whose support has been instrumental in my professional life.

Stage One:

Moral Considerations as Foundations

Chapter I

Moral Considerations

You are an employee of a government agency charged with maintaining highways. You have discovered that a number of administrators have received expensive gifts from certain contractors who routinely seek contracts to perform needed road repairs. These contractors are awarded the vast majority of road projects even though there are other businesses that could perform the work at least as well and at slightly less expense. After you talk to your superiors, it appears that nothing will be done about this arrangement. Should you inform a local newspaper or another government agency that will investigate the possibility of corruption?

You are a business executive. You have just learned that one of your plants is emitting a chemical that has recently been linked to lung cancer. There is currently no government regulation covering this pollutant, though the government has opened an investigation that is expected to lead to regulations in the future. Should you urge your company to institute costly measures to cut emissions — even before the government requires it? Should you urge efforts to see that the regulations are as weak as possible? Should you cooperate with the government's investigation?

The situations above raise serious moral problems — problems that cannot be solved simply be reciting standard moral principles. We can easily generate rules such as "One ought not threaten the health of others!" We can even uncover special obligations that emerge with different roles, for example, the obligation of public officials to award contracts fairly or the obligation of business executives to make profits for stockholders. But how do we proceed when one rule or obligation clashes with another, as when the business executive must decide between preventing threats to people's health and making profits for stockholders? To deal with these dilemmas, we need an understanding of the basis for the competing rules and of how to weigh and compare them. In other words, we need to understand the nature of moral analysis.

Moral analysis can be divided into three broad stages or levels: foundations, action guides, and applications. Our first experiences with morality occur at the second stage. As children, we learn what morality demands through rules such as those against killing and stealing. These rules explain our general moral obligations. They constitute guides to action. In almost all cases, to act correctly is to act according to whatever rules apply to the situation at hand.[1]

Still, it is not hard to uncover cases in which it is appropriate to violate certain moral action guides. The rule against stealing, for example, may be broken if the only way to get life-saving medical supplies for accident victims is by breaking into a locked store. Even the rule against killing can be legitimately violated if the only way to save the life of an innocent party is by killing an attacker. These exceptional cases, however, do not threaten the general rules. The rule against killing does not disappear because someone justifiably kills in self-defense. Rather, we say that the rule is *in certain, very special situations* outweighed by other relevant factors.

In other words, we distinguish between *action guides* (the general rules) and *judgments* about specific cases. This distinction marks the division between the second and third stages of moral analysis. The second stage provides guides for decision-making, but those guides must then be applied to specific cases. The applications represent the third stage of moral analysis. In most cases, the application is easy; there are few situations that require long deliberation about whether killing is permissible. But what should we say about abortion, where the obligation against killing points against such procedures while the obligation to allow persons to control their own bodies points toward permitting abortions? The issue in the abortion debate does not concern whether these obligations exist (i.e., whether there are action guides against killing or against interfering with people's choices). The issue is how to apply, weigh, and decide between them in a particular case, at stage three of moral analysis.

Such weighing and analysis requires an understanding of the nature of moral action guides, their content, and their basis. This last issue leads back to the first stage of moral analysis: the foundations for morality. Where do moral obligations come from? On what basis do they gain their force? For each of us, the original answer to both of these questions is likely to be some authority figure. Parents, religious leaders, and police (representing the law) transmit and enforce the rules in various ways. But appeal to others to explain the basis of morality is insufficient, for why did those individuals decide on the specific rules they support? Indeed, even if one appeals to God as the ultimate authority, why did God command that people not kill?

These are not idle questions. Every child will, at some point, question the foundation for a rule that is imposed by others. Even adults, when faced with a serious dilemma or a strong temptation to break a rule, will ask what makes the rule forceful. When the question "Why must I do that?" is raised, the answer sought is not an account of who gave the rule but an explanation of the *reasons for* the rule, the factors that make the rule an appropriate guide for behavior. It is these factors that provide the ultimate foundation for the rule and that represent the first stage of moral analysis. I will call these foundations 'moral considerations,' that is, factors that must be taken into account when moral questions are raised.

This chapter deals with the first task of moral analysis, the examination of moral considerations. As a provisional account, a consideration can be counted as a moral one if it is based on a regard for human beings in general — as opposed to a regard for one's own interests or for the law or for religious beliefs. (In Chapter V, I will indicate how this account of moral considerations is incomplete, for the factors developed for human beings can also be applied to other beings.) The provisional account, though broad, does provide a program for initial discussions about morality. We must discover those factors important to a human existence. Such considerations will represent expressions of our moral values. These values provide the basis for the moral action guides that underlie and justify actions. People avoid killing (specific actions) and claim to have an obligation not to kill (guide) because of the importance of human life (consideration) and the resulting value that is accorded such life.

The three stages of moral analysis can be summarized, in their proper order, as follows:

1. Foundations: the examination of the bases of moral analysis (that is, moral considerations),

2. Action Guides: the development of general moral obligations (for example, do not kill), and

3. Applications: the application of general obligations to specific types of acts (for example, whether abortion, as a medical procedure, is permissible) or to particular actions (for example, whether a specific person ought to have an abortion).

The first step in an analysis of morality is to articulate the various considerations that provide the foundation for moral obligations.

1. Preliminaries: Features of Human Nature

David Hume notes that the virtue of justice arises because of features of the human condition. Hume asks us to suppose that nature had provided human beings with an abundance of external goods such that every being could, without effort, provide itself with everything it desired. In such a situation, it seems that justice would be unnecessary, "For what purpose make a partition of goods when one has already more than enough? What give rise to property when there cannot possibly be any injury?"[2]

Hume's emphasis is on the external environment, the ease with which goods can be procured. An essential component of the story, however, concerns human nature: the interests of the people Hume depicts are such that the goods found ready-make in the natural environment are sufficient to satisfy all desires. If humans were the type of being that could flourish on what could be found within arms' reach, many moral principles would be unnecessary and, as Hume notes, "would never once have been dreamed of."[3]

Clearly, we do not live in a world in which all our wants and needs are easily satisfied; we are not the sort of being that can flourish without effort. "Hence the ideas of property become necessary in civil society; hence justice derives its usefulness to the public."[4] Hume speaks specifically of issues in ownership and distribution, but similar points can be made concerning other aspects of morality.

If we expand on the idea that our wants, needs, and abilities play a large role in determining how easily nature provides us with goods, it becomes clear that much of our morality is related to the type of being we are. If human life were not such a fragile commodity, if we were immortal, injunctions against murder might be unnecessary. If we did not rely on communication in forming beliefs and deciding how to act, lying might not be a moral issue.

The relationship between moral judgments and facts about human beings is hardly startling. Yet the connection does point to an important foundation for philosophical discussions of morality. If we are to understand the considerations that form the basis for an informed moral outlook, we must look to facts about human nature. This point is emphasized in the provisional account of moral considerations provided earlier: A consideration is a moral one if it relates to human beings in general. The capacities and limits of human beings provide the basis for our moral values.

Human nature can be viewed from two perspectives. On the one hand, we are living, physical beings with basic biological and emotional needs; on the other hand, we are active, thinking, conscious beings, able to determine our own goals and actions. Each perspective raises important moral considerations. An analysis of humans as living, physical beings raises many of the points noted in Hume's discussion. We have need for food and shelter from the elements. Our particular human situation makes clothing necessary in certain climates or in certain times of year. (In mild areas, clothing is still necessary, but for social and legal reasons.) Given the type of world we live in, such needs are not easily fulfilled. Food must be cultivated and prepared; clothing must be made. Building shelters requires great effort and many resources. Not only must human beings work to provide themselves with the necessities, but each person is dependent on a great many others for the basic requirements of life. We are, as the ancient Greeks noted well, social animals.

We are social beings in a further sense. Human beings have a variety of emotional needs, for affection, love, and companionship. Humans are also capable of a variety of pleasures — physical, emotional, aesthetic, and intellectual. There are pleasures in sexual activity, in listening to a beautiful symphony, even in hearing a good lecture. As rather sophisticated physical beings, we have a wide range of needs and desires, the fulfillment of which requires the cooperation of others.

On the other hand, human beings are also rational, conscious beings who can act on their own. Though dependent on others for physical and emotional needs, each person also maintains a degree of independence or autonomy. Language, reasoning ability, intellectual and locomotive skills, and foresight enable people, to make individual choices. Human beings can perceive personal goals and options, can relate various options and determine a best one, and can translate the choice into action.

The description of human beings as rational agents or choosers has a long history. Jean-Jacques Rousseau spoke of the perfectibility of human beings, by which he meant the ability of people through their own choices, to develop new skills and new ways of accomplishing goals.[5] John Locke's political writings, like those of many other supporters of democratic government, emphasize the human capacity to will, which is the ability to make decisions for oneself.[6] Indeed, many persons have argued that the ability to think and to choose is a significant difference between human beings and other animals.

Leaving aside the question of whether animals can choose, it seems clear that human beings can decide on a personal life style and on what to do with their lives — and generally have the ability to act on these decisions. In the course of deciding and acting on these questions, each human being has some ability to determine what sort of person he or she will be.

2. *Two Moral Theories*

The two perspectives on human nature can be linked to two views of morality, that is, two views of what considerations and strategies are crucial in moral decision-making. Utilitarian theories emphasize the satisfaction of needs and wants humans have as living, physical beings. Deontological theories concentrate on respect for human choices. As we will see, neither theory *must* limit itself to only one of the perspectives on human nature. Because of differing assessments of the human condition, however, early accounts of each theory tended to focus on a single type of moral consideration.

Jeremy Bentham defended the principle of utility as the criterion for moral action. For Bentham, morality is a matter of weighing the effects of one's actions in order to maximize happiness and minimize unhappiness. "By the principle of utility is meant that principle which approves or disapproves of every action whatsoever, according to the tendency which it appears to have to augment or diminish the happiness of the party whose interest is in question."[7] In other words, an action is morally correct if its effects yield or produce the greatest balance of total happiness over harmful consequences. An act of killing someone to gain an inheritance is not morally acceptable since, even though I would be happier if I had the money now, the increase in happiness for me is outweighed by the harmful effects to the victim. To cause someone's death is generally the worst thing that can be done to a person.

Bentham claims that it is needless to prove the principle of utility, for it is the starting point for moral deliberations. It is used to prove all other points of morality. But the principle provides such a starting point because of the way humans are built. As Bentham notes, "By the natural constitution of the human frame, on most occasions of their lives men in general embrace this principle, without thinking of it."[8] Still, it is necessary to elaborate the principle.

To determine just what considerations fall under the principle of utility, Bentham develops a specific account of happiness. Happiness is considered equivalent to pleasure; the search for pleasures and the avoidance of pain serve as the primary, even the only motivations for human action.

> Nature has placed mankind under the governance of two sovereign masters, *pain* and *pleasure*. It is for them alone to point out what we ought to do, as well as to determine what we shall do. On the one hand the standard of right and wrong, on the other the chain of causes and effects, are fastened to their throne. They govern us in all we do, in all we say, in all we think: every effort we can make to throw off our subjection, will serve but to demonstrate and confirm it.[9]

Such talk indicates how much Bentham's moral theory concentrates on the fact that human beings are physical entities with consequent wants and needs. We are "natural" beings, "governed" by, even "under the subjection of," pleasure and pain. To determine what constitutes moral considerations, it is necessary to look no further than the pleasure and pains that humans are subjected to, for example, those of the senses, of friendship, and of power.[10]

To resolve moral problems, one must, on Bentham's view, consider what sorts of pleasures and pains would be produced for *each* person affected by possible actions. To accomplish this, Bentham describes a detailed procedure.

I. For each person affected:

1 . consider the value of each *pleasure* (likely to be) *directly* produced by the act in question[11]

2 . consider the value of each *pain* (likely to be) *directly* produced by the act

3 . consider the value of each *pleasure* (likely to be) *indirectly* produced by the act

4 . consider the value of each *pain* (likely to be) *indirectly* produced by the act

5 . sum up all the pleasures and pains and determine the balance.

II. When the above calculations have been completed, add up the totals for each person affected. If the total has a balance of pleasure over pain, the act tends to improve utility. If the total has a sum of pain over pleasure, the act yields disutility.[12]

As the principle of utility implies, the correct action is the one that maximizes the balance of pleasure (happiness) over pain (harmful consequences).

In opposition to Bentham, Immanuel Kant develops an account of morality that minimizes the importance of physical and emotional needs. Happiness, as Bentham described it, concerns human needs and desires. For Kant, these factors represent inclinations. As nonrational features of human nature, they are irrelevant to morality. Morality concerns our duties, what we ought to do, as opposed to what we want or are inclined to do. I may desperately want a particular tape deck, but whether or not my stealing it would maximize happiness, I have a duty not to steal it. I act correctly when I fulfill my obligations or duties simply because they are my duties.

What Kant must explain is where moral duties come from. Morality is an issue for human beings because they are capable of deliberating and deciding how to act. We can decide whether and when to act on desires; we are not simply subject to physical inclinations. The capacity that enables us to do this is our ability to reason. Of course, we do not always follow what reason tells us; people often have too many beers even though they know they shouldn't. But we do have the capacity to use our reason to decide what we *ought* to do, and then we can act on the decision. Kant's view begins with an emphasis on aspects of human nature associated with rationality and choice. We are conscious, rational agents or choosers.

For Kant, then, it is reason that determines what our duties are. If we looked simply to our desires and interests, we might find many cases in which even killing could be justified. Suppose I was in great need of money to support my family and would receive a sizeable inheritance on the death of a sad, old, arthritic uncle who is "just waiting to die." In weighing the utilitarian consequences, I might find that my family would gain much more than my uncle would lose if he were killed. Still, the killing seems wrong. Kant would defend this intuition by arguing that what is crucial to morality is not the consequences of actions but the nature of the action itself. There is something wrong with the act of killing — pulling the trigger with the intention of taking a human life — no matter how good the consequences are.

It is not surprising, then, that Kant considers the will, the ability to make rational choices, as the only thing that can be good in itself. "It is impossible," he says, "to conceive of anything at all in the world, or even out of it, which can be taken as good without qualification, except a *good will*."[13] Other things, like intelligence or wealth, are good only if used properly, that is, only if used by a person who chooses — or wills — properly. A good will would always fulfill its rational duties.

But what would reason, devoid of desires or inclinations, demand? To see this, let us consider what seems wrong about killing an aging uncle for an inheritance. As noted above, weighing the effects of the action on happiness may justify killing, but it ignores a very different type of value, the value that the uncle has as a being capable of directing his own life, of deciding and acting on his own choices. As a conscious, rational agent, the uncle has value as an individual and is owed the freedom to make his own choices.

These values of freedom and individual worth represent the foundations for Kant's moral system. They generate the fundamental principle or action guide for Kantian ethics. One way Kant formulates this fundamental rule is, "Act in such a way that you always treat humanity, whether in your own person or the person of another, never simply as a means, but always at the same time as an end."[14] Killing the uncle is wrong according to this principle because it involves treating him as a means to money and not as an end, a being worthy of respect. Kant calls this supreme principle of morality a categorical imperative, that is, a command or law of reason that is upheld independently of any interest or inclination that might be furthered by acting on it.

Kant claims that the rule presented above is equivalent to another formulation of the categorical imperative, namely, "Act only on that maxim through which you can at the same time will that it should become a universal law."[15] A somewhat simpler version might be, "Act according to rules that one can accept as universal laws." All human beings, as rational choosers, have absolute value and must be respected for what they are. One accomplishes this by acting, in any situation, on that rule which all rational beings would accept and follow, that is, by acting on universal moral laws.

Kant's approach to ethics captures an important sense of personal integrity. This is often described in terms of acting on principle — even if such action requires personal sacrifices. Kant's avoidance of considerations of happiness or desire is consistent with this. One acts out of respect for persons, no matter what the consequences. If treating persons as ends requires telling officials the truth about an employer's transgressions, then one must do so — even if this will mean harms to co-workers and the loss of one's job.

A number of familiar moral rules can be derived from Kant's supreme principle. Kant himself develops rules against killing oneself and others, lying, and stealing. Lying, for example, is wrong because it interferes with the ability of persons to make judgments and choices and, thus, (1) could not be willed as a universal law and (2) involves treating people as a means to one's own ends. For Kant, moral considerations relate to respect for the rational side of human nature. One ought not cut off options, provide incorrect information, or otherwise restrict the ability of people to act as rational agents.

3. Criticisms of the Two Views

Since Bentham and Kant purport to present complete views of morality, their theories deal with all three stages in moral analysis, from foundations, to action guides, to applications. If we interpret their views very strictly, much can be learned about moral considerations.

	Strict Utilitarianism	Strict Deontological Theory
Moral Considerations	Human Welfare and Happiness (in its various aspects)	Human Freedom and the Intrinsic Worth of Rational Beings
Action Guides	Act to maximize the total happiness of all persons affected by the action (The Principle of Utility)	Act on universal rules of duty (rules consistent with treating persons as ends, as beings worthy of respect for what they are)
Applications	General Strategy: In any situation, uncover all the consequences for happiness, weigh and compute the total impact of each option on happiness, choose the option that best satisfies the principle of utility	General Strategy: Consider each act in itself and whether the rule governing the act could qualify as a universal law (which indicates a respect for rational beings)
	Specific Example: Killing a healthy, happy person to gain an inheritance (simply to avoid working) is wrong because the harm to the victim outweighs the benefits to the killer.	Specific Example: Lying to a friend to avoid embarrassment is wrong because it indicates a lack of respect for the friend as a moral agent who relies on correct information.

The action guides and applications outlined for each view follow from the type of consideration emphasized. Bentham's reliance on maximizing total happiness is a natural outgrowth of his description of moral considerations in terms of human welfare. Kant's emphasis on universal rules that respect persons as ends emerges from his account of the worth of rational beings as choosers. The obligations developed represent a way to make the considerations effective in deliberations and actions. Problems with the results that emerge from applications of the obligations may indicate difficulties in the respective accounts of moral considerations.

It is important to note that in most cases Bentham and Kant will agree on the morally correct action. In general, both philosophers will consider killing, stealing, and lying wrong. Each view can answer most of the easy questions concerning what actions are morally correct. But if a moral theory is to be helpful, it must provide guidance in hard cases.

As might be expected, however, strict utilitarian and deontological views are not always helpful. Kant can be questioned for a too-heavy reliance on principles that do not permit exception. Bentham can be criticized for overemphasizing the welfare of the whole against the legitimate interests of the individual. This was evident in the example indicating that a utilitarian justification for killing one's uncle could be given if the death would benefit many others.

Consider the following example in light of a strict utilitarian theory. Suppose a very close friend is debating which of two companies to work for. Company A offers a significantly higher salary; but, given your experience with A, you believe that job will be less beneficial, less secure, and will offer less chance of advancement. You strongly recommend the offer from company B and believe your friend would make a serious mistake by joining A. After hearing all of this, your friend is still inclined to take the extra money and to worry about the future later. On a strict utilitarian perspective, if you (justifiably) believe that your friend is making a wrong decision and that he or she would be much better off joining B, you have an obligation to induce your friend to pick B. If the truth is not adequate to the task, it is perfectly appropriate, even necessary, for you to invent horror stories about working for A so that your friend will choose B.

Most of us would say that such tactics go too far, and the reasons are likely to have a Kantian tone. The decision on which job to take is, after all, your friend's. It is his or her life, and if, after weighing all the relevant evidence, he or she is interested in taking the higher paying job even though it may well prove to be a mistake, that choice ought to be respected. The problem for strict utilitarianism is that in weighing consequences in terms of human well-being or happiness, the importance and worth of the actions themselves are not considered. Yet, there is something very special about the ability of people to decide for themselves — even if the decisions sometimes turn out to be less than the best. A strict utilitarian view does not have adequate room for respect for people as rational agents.

While a strict deontologist recognizes the need to respect human beings as agents, such a view cannot account for situations in which physical needs seem to take precedence over respect for people. Consider the following case: You witness a serious auto accident; the driver of a car loses control and rams a wall. The driver and passenger appear to be seriously hurt. Unfortunately, the scene of the accident is a remote rural area with just a few shops to service travelers. All of those shops are now closed. You can and do use a public phone to call for medical help, but this will not arrive for some time, and it is not clear that the victims will survive that period without some medical aid. You could provide such aid; unfortunately, you have no medical supplies. There are medical supplies in one of the stores, but it is locked and deserted. To save the lives, you break into the store and take the needed materials.

A strict deontologist may contend that your actions are clearly and unequivocally wrong. There are, after all, a number of persons to consider. Clearly the victims' chances of survival seem to depend on the supplies, but these people can make no claim to the goods. To take the supplies would amount to stealing, that is, taking the store owner's property without consent. One would be treating the store owner simply as a means to a goal. To be sure, the goal of saving a life is an important one, but one must never treat an individual as a means only, no matter what the goal.

This does not mean that a strict deontologist would advocate ignoring the accident victims. One should try to save the lives, but there are limits on permissible ways to accomplish this. No goal can ever override our moral duty to respect all human beings as ends. If we discover a goal that cannot be accomplished without violating this fundamental precept, then we must accept that the goal will not be achieved. If the accident victims' lives cannot be saved without stealing the supplies, we must (after doing what is permissible to save them) accept the deaths as unfortunate but unpreventable.

But the situation concerning accident victims seems to present a very special case. Lives were at stake, and the store owner's medical supplies were the only means of the victims' survival. In such cases, a consideration of the consequences for human welfare is essential. As Bentham would argue, the store owner loses very little compared to the great benefits that are gained by the victims if the supplies are taken. Cases in which severe, harmful consequences are likely may provide legitimate exceptions to common rules. A strict deontological theory cannot account for these cases because they raise considerations that do not fit such a system. Human beings are not just rational agents; they have physical needs and wants. Morality must take account of these.

As a result, fundamental criticisms of strict utilitarian and deontological theories deal with their starting points. Since each theory depends on an assessment of the human condition that emphasizes one side to human nature, each is likely to miss some crucial moral considerations. Strict utilitarian and deontological views are inadequate on their own. The reason each view is defective, however, is that each failed to incorporate the considerations deemed essential by the other. In determining what the fundamental moral considerations are, both views must be taken into account.

4. Developing a Complete Account of Moral Considerations

The criticisms presented above have not been ignored by theorists in either the utilitarian or the deontological tradition. Indeed, though Bentham and Kant did present rather extreme views, neither would completely ignore the moral consideration defended by the other. Bentham's utilitarianism was directed largely toward legislative reform, and in these areas, he upheld some of the points Kant emphasized. Bentham strongly defended liberty of the press and of public discussion.[16] To be sure, his defense of freedom was strictly utilitarian: to serve as a check on government and to provide information so that beneficial decisions would be made. Still, though the value of freedom is explained in utilitarian terms, certain types of freedom are important to Bentham.

While Bentham found some place for freedom in his system, Kant was not oblivious to the physical needs of human beings. When morality is applied to humans, duties that involve what Betham might call promoting happiness arise. Consider Kant's discussion of charity: "Charity to one's fellows should be commended rather as a debt of honor than as an exhibition of kindness and generosity."[17] The duty of charity is a special instance of the general duty of beneficence: "to be helpful to men in need according to one's means, for the sake of their happiness and without hope for anything thereby."[18] This is a universal duty because other human beings must be regarded as "needy rational beings, united by nature in one dwelling place for mutual aid."[19] It is important to note that such duties, unlike duties not to kill, steal, and lie, have a qualification included based on one's means; and it is not clear that duties of beneficence could provide exceptions to unqualified duties like that against stealing. To a limited extent, however, the views of Kant and Bentham do include considerations arising from both sides of human nature.

Many utilitarian and deontological thinkers who followed Bentham and Kant have futher combined both types of moral consideration. John Stuart Mill, perhaps the foremost utilitarian philosopher, also wrote an extremely important defense of individual liberty.[20] Sir David Ross's emphasis on duties and the idea that actions can be valuable in themselves (independently of their consequences) places him in the deontological tradition. Yet he still enumerates many duties that take account of the utilitarian emphasis on happiness and that leave room for the sorts of exceptions strict deontological theories could not handle.[21]

Utilitarian views can be made more acceptable by developing a fuller account of human happiness. Happiness is not simply a matter of feeling physical or emotional pleasures, it is also a matter of developing and exercising talents, of establishing and acting on goals, of determining what sort of person one wishes to be and of acting on such ideals. For these activities, one must be left free to make one's own decisions and to develop one's individuality. The value of individuality is eloquently defended by Mill.

It is not by wearing down into uniformity all that is individual in themselves, but by cultivating it, and calling it forth, within the limits imposed by the rights and interests of others, that human beings become a noble and beautiful object of contemplation.[22]

Indeed, with respect to cases such as that concerning your friend's decision about job offers, Mill, siding with Kant, notes

[Your friend] cannot rightfully be compelled to do or forbear because it will be better for him to do so, because it will make him happier, because, in the opinion of others, to do so would be wise, or even right. These are good reasons for remonstrating with him, for reasoning with him, or persuading him, or entreating him, but not for compelling him, or visiting him with any evil in case he do otherwise.[23]

How are such claims about upholding individual freedom even when happiness might be negatively affected to be made consistent with utilitarianism? Many persons have claimed Mill was not consistent here. But in *On Liberty*, Mill spends a section describing individuality and control over one's person as an element of well-being and happiness. He states that "utility in the largest sense, is grounded in the permanent interests of man as a progressive being."[24]

In areas in which others are not harmed, Mill speaks of the value of individual diversity. Only by developing their talents and interests can individuals foster originality and advance over past knowledge and practices. As he puts it, "the only unfailing and permanent source of improvement is liberty."[25]

The importance of individual freedom and moral rules like those elaborated by Kant is reaffirmed in *Utilitarianism*, where Mill explicitly defines and defends his utilitarianism. He points out the central importance of obligations to avoid harms, such as killing and stealing, and to respect the freedom of individuals. He even describes these moral rules as being of "more paramount obligation" than any others. Mill, of course, believes these rules are ultimately grounded in the principle of utility, but this once again indicates (1) how broadly he interprets the happiness that must be promoted and (2) how consistent Mill thinks moral rules (of the type described by Kant) can be with utilitariansim.[26] Mill the utilitarian has managed to incorporate considerations associated with both sides of human nature.

Deontological theories can accomplish the same feat. Ross clearly upholds certain basic tenets of the deontological tradition. He refutes the claim that actions are right in so far as they maximize happiness. In determining the correctness of an act, Ross looks to the past (to the duties present at the time of the act) rather than to the future (to the consequences of the act). Like Kant, he considers the action itself and its relation to duty.

Recall, however, that Kant's emphasis on universal rules as the foundation for duty made it difficult to recognize exceptions even when human welfare would demand it. Ross softens Kant's account of the foundations for duties. Ross speaks of *prima facie* duties, that is, moral obligations that are not absolute and can be outweighed by other moral obligations, depending on the circumstances. In terms of the stages of moral analysis, prima facie duties clearly function at the second stage, as action guides. If prima facie duties clash when applied to specific situations (in the third stage of moral analysis), it is necessary for people to deliberate and to come to a considered judgment about which is most important.

Ross further develops the deontological perspective by expanding the types of considerations that can qualify as prima facie duties. Recall Kant's principle requiring that humanity — in oneself and others — be respected (or treated as an end). For Kant, what was ultimately worthy of respect was the rational will of human beings. But since humans are also physical beings, it is not unreasonable to extend respect for humanity to include respect for persons not only as choosers but also as physical beings with biological and emotional needs. Ross notes: "Just as before we were led to recognize the *prima facie* rightness of the fulfillment of promises, we are now led to recognize the *prima facie* rightness by promoting the general welfare."[27] Here, Ross extends the scope of obligations and duties to cases of upholding the utilitarian consideration of promoting happiness or the general welfare. Since Ross describes all basic moral duties in prima facie terms, the duty to promote the general welfare can be as significant as any other. Thus, for Ross, there may be good reasons to take the needed medical supplies. Certainly the general welfare is greatly increased by such action. Though taking the supplies might technically be described as stealing, in this case, the prima facie duty to promote the general welfare can outweigh the prima facie duty not the steal. Ross, then, can incorporate utilitarian considerations in a deontological system.

The above discussions indicate that on the subject of what considerations are important, utilitarian and deontological thinkers can be brought close to agreement. Utilitarians will include under human happiness not only considerations of human welfare or pleasures but also considerations of human freedom and respect for choice. Deontologists will include under respect for humanity not only considerations of human freedom and respect for people as individual rational beings but also considerations of human welfare. Each side has come to recognize the importance of the two types of moral considerations. The reason for this convergence is clear. Since morality deals with the way human beings ought to be treated and since human beings have reasoning and decision-making capacities as well as physical needs and wants, any account of the proper treatment of such beings must take account of humans both as individual choosers and as physical beings who must work to survive.

My purpose has not been to show that utilitarian and deontological theories are the same. Clearly they are not. As the early discussions of Bentham and Kant indicated, there are significant points of disagreement: over the relative importance of actions themselves as opposed to the consequences of actions, over the role and importance of moral rules, over the basic principle of morality, and over the strategies for determining proper actions. The previous discussions, however, have focused on issues that are, in many respects, prior to questions of rules, principles, and strategies. The issues examined here concern what factors must be taken into account when dealing with moral questions: what factors lead to moral rules and principles and are to be weighed by moral strategies.

Here, despite surface differences, there are significant similarities between utilitarian and deontological theories. As the discussions of Mill and Ross indicated, utilitarians and deontologists include in their moral theories considerations associated with both human welfare and individual freedom. Concern for freedom and welfare provide the heart, the basis of theories of morality.

Such a conclusion should not be surprising, for considerations of welfare and freedom naturally arise from an examination of human nature. In searching for the factors that relate to human beings in

general, the two sides to human nature must be included. Each type
of theory, in its own way, attempts to do just that.

5. The Objectivity of Moral Considerations

Since welfare and freedom represent factors that are important to
human beings simply because of the type of being they are, these
considerations provide an objective basis for morality. These moral
considerations were not derived from personal feelings or opinions
that may vary from person to person. Rather, the foundations for
moral analysis emerged from the characteristics, capacities, and needs
of human beings as a species. People cannot avoid the conclusion that
the general features of basic biological and emotional well-being and
the freedom to make individual choices that they value are also valued
by others.

This is not to say that everyone has the same opinion of what
counts as welfare and the appropriate realms of freedom. One person
may view happiness in terms of family activities; another might
emphasize career development. Indeed, one might value life over any
religious commitment, while another would willingly sacrifice
physical existence in order to follow religious dictates. Indeed, the
importance of freedom can be described in terms of the ability to
develop and to act on a personal conception of well-being. Yet each
person will have a view of human welfare that weaves, in different
ways, the general but settled features associated with human happiness. Each person's view of happiness will be developed within the
limits presented by human nature.

The view that morality rests on objective foundations has been
defended by philosophers from the time of the ancient Greeks. One
common way to defend the objectivity of morality mirrors the
strategy for developing moral considerations. The key is to uncover
important similarities among human beings. Since general needs to
welfare and freedom are common to people, these values and considerations are objective in the sense that they apply to human beings
regardless of personal beliefs, feelings, or attitudes. The claim that the
foundations of morality are objective need imply no more.

6. Conclusion

It is time to take stock. We began with the task of discovering what counts as a moral consideration, that is, what factors must be taken into account when dealing with moral issues. This led to an analysis of the general features of human nature, which yielded two broad types of considerations: (1) human welfare considerations and (2) human freedom considerations.

It is important to remember that since moral considerations must have general applicability, moral concerns for *human* freedom and *human* welfare are different from self-interested concerns for *personal* well-being. People take a special interest in their own particular needs or interests. Each individual may seek to get a good job and to make a reasonable wage. These self-interested concerns are not necessarily morally unacceptable. A special interest in one's own well-being can often be consistent with moral demands. The key feature of moral considerations, however, is that they range beyond personal interests to the interests of all individuals. (A number of issues concerning the relationship between self-interest and morality will be examined in Chapter IV.)

Here, I want simply to summarize the moral side, the factors that can be included under the general heading of welfare and freedom considerations. The following list is not meant to be conclusive.

Considerations of Human Welfare (and the various aspects of human happiness)	*Considerations of Human Freedom (and the worth of people — rational beings — as unique choosers)*
Physical survival (in terms of health, use of limbs)	Decision making abilities, in terms of:
Physical well-being (e.g., absense of pains, opportunities for physical comforts like sex, exercise)	Development of options (e.g., through educational training, equal access to jobs and resources)

Considerations of Human Welfare (and the various aspects of human happiness)	*Considerations of Human Freedom (and the worth of people — rational beings — as unique choosers)*
Emotional or psychological well-being (e.g., absence of phobias, ability to function in reality, satisfaction of emotional needs)	Ability to deliberate and to decide (e.g., having proper information — through truth-telling)
Aesthetic and intellectual pleasures (e.g., musical and dramatic performances, learning how the solar system works)	Ability to carry out decisions (e.g., absence of force, threats, or other interference)
	Uniqueness of people, in terms of (1) diversity of interests, styles, attitudes, and abilities and (2) personal contributions

These considerations, as foundations for moral analysis, will provide the basis for the rules and principles that must be analyzed when specific moral problems are dealt with.

Many of those moral problems will involve clashes of welfare and freedom considerations. Parents often must decide between doing what they truly believe is good for a child (welfare considerations) and respecting what they believe is a bad but firm decision by the child (freedom considerations). Physicians may grapple with similar issues in the treatment of patients. Is it ever permissible to dupe a patient into consenting to a simple but necessary operation which the patient has refused because of what appears to be undue anxiety over surgery?

There is no easy solution to these questions. The difficulties arise in part because the factors that must be compared are so different. We can, as the utilitarians suggest, make rough judgments about relative welfare gains; but there is no analogous procedure for comparing gains in welfare to losses of freedom. We must sort through the details of each problem, uncovering and evaluating the general guides at issue, and carefully — perhaps agonizingly — deliberating to a judgment.

Such deliberations, however, occur at the third stage of moral analysis: applications. There, the ultimate issue is not what factors provide the basis for moral discussions — though one may have to deal with this question in order to solve the problem one is facing — but the application of the relevant features. How ought the conflicting considerations and guides be related and weighed? The discussions in this chapter have only concerned issues at stage one: the discovery of what factors count as moral considerations. Welfare, freedom, and worth considerations will provide substantial foundations for the analysis of difficult moral problems.

Notes

1. Rules and principles represent the most obvious type of action guide, but virtues and rights fall into this category as well. As states of character or dispositions to act in certain ways, virtues provide strong guidance for action. I will speak briefly of the virtues in Chapter IV and of rights in Chapter VI. Our discussions will concentrate on guides such as rules and principles, however, since these explicit statements of moral demands are more easily raised in deliberations about specific moral problems.

2. David Hume, *An Enquiry concerning the Principles of Morals*, in *Hume's Moral and Political Philosophy*, ed. Henry D. Aiken (New York: Hafner Publishing Co., 1972), p. 185.

3. Hume, p. 185.

4. Hume, p. 189.

5. See Jean-Jacques Rousseau, *Discourse on the Origin and Foundations of Inequality among Men*, Part 1.

6. See especially Locke's *Second Treatise on Government*.

7. Jeremy Bentham, *Introduction to the Principles of Morals and Legislation*, in *The Works of Jeremy Bentham*, 6 Vols. (Edinburgh: William Tait Co., 1843), I:1.

8. Bentham, I:2.

9. Bentham, I:1.

10. Bentham lists a number of pleasures and pains; see Bentham, I:17.

11. Note that the *value* of a pleasure or pain will be affected by its likelihood and directness. The less likely a pleasure, the less value it will have in the calculations. In addition, factors such as the intensity and duration of pleasures must be considered.

12. See Bentham, p. 16.

13. Immanuel Kant, *Groundwork of the Metaphysic of Morals* (New York: Harper and Row, Harper Torchbook 1956), p. 61.

14. Kant, p. 96.

15. Kant, p. 88. This is actually the first formulation Kant presents. The rule concerning treating persons as ends is Kant's second formulation. He develops a third formulation. See Kant, pp. 100–104.

16. See Bentham, *On Liberty of Press and Public Discussion*, in *The Works of Jeremy Bentham*, Vol. II.

17. Immanuel Kant, *Lectures on Ethics* (New York: Harper and Row, Harper Torchbooks, 1963), p. 236.

18. Immanual Kant, *The Metaphysical Principles of Virtue* (Indianapolis, Ind.: Bobbs-Merrill Co., Library of Liberal Arts, 1964), p. 117.

19. Kant, *The Metaphysical Principles of Virtue*, p. 117.

20. See John Stuart Mill, *On Liberty* and *Utilitarianism*, in *Utilitarianism, Liberty, and Representative Government* (New York: E.P. Dutton and Co., Everyman's Library, 1951).

21. See W.D. Ross, *The Right and the Good* (Oxford: Oxford University Press, The Clarendon Press, 1930).

22. Mill, *On Liberty*, p. 161.

23. Mill, *On Liberty*, p. 96.

24. Mill, *On Liberty*, p. 97.

25. Mill, *On Liberty*, p. 171.

26. In speaking of "more paramount obligation," Mill does leave room for exceptions. (See Mill, *Utilitarianism*, pp. 79–80.) But as noted in the discussions of Kant, exceptions seem necessary even with respect to crucially important moral rules.

27. Ross, p. 47.

Chapter II

Subjectivism, Relativism, and Morality

P opular views imply that morality has no firm foundation, that morals are based simply on personal feelings or social attitudes. Such views of morality naturally arise in a nation and a world as diverse as ours.

Consider the common image of the United States as a "melting pot." The idea implies that we are a country of many different nationalities, religions, races, and beliefs. As a result, our political and social institutions place great emphasis on tolerating and even encouraging diversity among individuals. This diversity extends to many moral beliefs. Individuals who uphold different religious doctrines, for example, may well make opposite judgments on a variety of moral questions, from abortion and capital punishment to premarital sex. Thus, it is natural for us to think that moral decisions are simply a matter of personal or group opinion.

In addition, we live in a world that is constantly brought closer together through satellite communications, complex trade relations, and the ease of traveling long distances. We are continuously made aware of the diversity in ideals and beliefs among cultures. Customs and laws vary markedly on issues ranging from the number of spouses an individual may take to the permissibility of euthanasia to the value of freedom of expression. Once again, we are led to consider moral judgments to be a matter of opinion or attitude or location.

It is difficult to deny that moral judgments differ from person to person and from society to society. And it certainly is not obvious that when disagreements occur, one side is correct and the other wrong. Often, each view has significant support. It is important, however, to understand the nature of this diversity. To say that individuals disagree about the morality of premarital sex means that individuals make different judgments about the permissibility of a particular action. Similarly, when cultures differ over policies like the death penalty, the dispute centers on a specific judgment. Both types of disagreement emerge at the third stage of moral analysis, the application of considerations and guides to particular cases.

In the previous chapter, the foundations of moral analysis, the basic considerations of welfare and freedom, were described as objective. This implies that moral considerations, the first stage of moral analysis, are not just a matter of personal or social belief, but are rooted in certain facts about the world and the place of our species in it. On the surface, there appears to be a contradiction in claiming that the foundations for morality are objective while at the same time recognizing that different people and cultures may legitimately make divergent judgments on particular moral issues. A major goal of this chapter is to show that there is no contradiction here, that objective foundations for morality can still yield divergent specific judgments.

Many people, however, accept the contradiction and contend that differences in specific judgments imply that there is no objective foundation for morality. To begin combatting this view, note that the complexity of the situations in which moral judgments are made can partially explain differences in particular judgments. Take, for instance, what appears to be the most simple and forceful of moral rules, "Do no kill!" Certainly, there are exceptions, the most obvious of which are self-defense or the defense of others. But though the rule and exceptions are quite clear as general guides to action, when applied in specific cases, numerous difficulties can arise. Consider unintended threats against someone's life, like a fetus whose continued existence is practically certain to lead to the bearer's death. Suppose now that the fetus is likely to, but may not, cause the bearer's death. Consider also the case of a thief who threatens someone with an empty gun — which is, as a result, no real threat. Perhaps a popular position would be that in each of these cases, killing in self-defense would be justified. But some people would disagree, arguing, for example, that it is not proper to take the life of someone who is completely innocent. The examples cited above do not exhaust the complexities associated with the applications of a rule against killing. The controversy over whether it is permissible to kill a person in a deep and irreversible coma raises very different problems. It is not surprising that individuals, societies, and religious traditions have developed different answers to some of these questions.

Nothing about morality implies that each moral question can have only one correct answer. There may be a range of morally permissible actions, and many differences in moral judgments may fall within this range. If what counts as a good moral reason must be the same for all parties, that is, if there is a set of moral considerations that must be appealed to in moral analysis, then morality cannot be *just* a matter of personal or social attitudes. Rather, moral analysis will be a deliberative activity involving the development of an acceptable system of judgments from common foundations.

To support this perspective on morality, it is necessary to examine the arguments for thinking that there are no objective foundations for moral analysis. I do not want to deny any personal or social influences on moral judgments. Rather, I will seek to demonstrate the untenability of the extreme claim that morality is nothing more than personal feeling or social attitudes. This discussion will proceed in two parts.

The first part will consider the claim that morality is just a matter of personal belief. I will call this view *subjectivism*, though it is important to remember that the version to be examined is an extreme form of subjectivism. My goal in this discussion will be to indicate how moral analysis is a rational activity.

The second part will consider the claim that morality is just a matter of social or cultural attitudes. I will call this view *relativism*. Again, the view to be discussed here is an extreme form. My analysis of relativism will uncover ways different judgments at the third stage of moral analysis can be based on similar foundations.

1. A Philosophical Defense of Subjectivism

Perhaps the strongest statement of a subjectivist view of ethics is presented by A.J. Ayer.[1] A number of other philosophers, for example,

C.L. Stevenson,[2] have further developed the type of position Ayer expounds. I will briefly explain Ayer's account of the view and some important embellishments provided by Stevenson. For Ayer, ethical judgments are just *expressions* of feelings. In describing the judgment "It was wrong that you stole the money," Ayer notes, "It is as if I had said, 'You stole that money,' in a particular tone of horror, or had written it with the addition of some special exclamation marks."[3]

Ayer observes that moral language may also be used to *arouse* feeling. To say something is wrong may — and may be intended to — lead others to feel disapproval. Of course, ethical judgments may not succeed in arousing the desired emotion, but the issue turns simply on whether or not the feeling does arise. This is the use of moral judgments that Stevenson emphasizes. "Their [ethical judgments'] major use is not to indicate facts but to *create* an influence."[4] Stevenson describes the use of moral judgments to generate reactions as a "dynamic" use. This use follows from the same basic point concerning ethical terms that Ayer emphasized. Ethical terms have an emotive meaning, that is, they express and create feelings.

It follows that ethical judgments do not state facts about the action being judged. There is nothing about the act that determines how an individual ought to react to it. In Ayer's terms, morality concerns just the feelings individuals happen to have about actions, and moral judgments are just one way of publicly expressing one's feelings. Note that Ayer has moved from an examination of ethical judgments, at stage three of moral analysis, to an explanation of morality itself as just a matter of individual feeling. In other words, Ayer describes the foundations for morality, stage one, in terms of each individual's emotional reaction to actions. Individuals will often make very different ethical judgments because different feelings have been aroused and are being expressed.

For Ayer, there is no such thing as an argument about values. Whenever we think we are debating values, we will find that the issue really concerns either the meaning of relevant terms or the facts of the case.

Suppose that two witnesses argue about the moral acceptability of one individual's attack on another. The discussion may focus on whether the person attacked did something sufficient to provoke it. The witnesses may argue over whether, in fact, the person attacked had drawn a knife. But if they agree over the fact that a knife was pulled but disagree about whether this is sufficient to warrant an attack, no further argument is possible. The witnesses have different reactions to the event, and that is the end of the argument.

Now, suppose that two individuals are arguing about whether it is permissible to kill for personal gain. The dispute may focus on what counts as personal gain. Here, people can argue about what terms should mean. However, if these people agree on the relevant terminology but disagree about whether killing in such cases is permissible, rational argument ends. The individuals have different reactions to specific cases, and that's the end of the debate. This need not mean that all discussion ends. Individuals may continue, through emotional appeals, to try to arouse the desired feeling or reaction in others. But there is no *rational* way to settle differences over values. Argument serves no purpose, since there are no facts left to argue over.

Thus, Ayer considers moral judgments to be radically different from ordinary statements of fact. If, in the scientific realm, I were to say that the earth is flat and you were to say that the earth is a sphere, our statements would contradict. We are speaking about the same thing; we are commenting about a feature of the world, and only one of the statements can be true. If, in the moral realm, I were to say that it is wrong to cheat and you were to say it is right to cheat, there is, on Ayer's view, no contradiction. Though it may appear that each of us is making a statement about the world at large and, thus, that only one of us can be correct, Ayer would warn us that these moral judgments do not represent statements about the act of cheating. Rather, the judgments express each individuals's feelings about cheating. For me to say it is wrong to cheat is just an expression of my adverse reaction to cheating and (perhaps) an attempt to generate a similar reaction in you. For you to say it is right to cheat is just an expression of your positive reaction to cheating and (perhaps) an attempt to generate a similar reaction in me.

Morality becomes a matter of taste, and we accept wide differences on matters of taste. There is no more sense to arguing about what is right or wrong than there would be in arguing about whether your preference for chocolate ice cream is better than my preference for vanilla. There can be no rational argument about which preference is better.

But in the moral realm, we want to do more. We are inclined to say that a person who condones killing to gain an inheritance not only has a different morality but has a wrong morality. And we are likely to give reasons for the claim, reasons that evoke earlier discussions of moral considerations. Killing is the most significant harm that can be done to people; it negates not only welfare but also the ability of people to carry out goals. Personal financial gain will not outweigh these considerations.

Similar arguments arise with respect to many pressing moral issues. The debate over whether the fetus qualifies as a human life is not a purely scientific or factual one. We can easily distinguish between a living fetus and a dead one, and either way, it has the genetic code that makes it biologically human. The issue is whether the fetus ought to be considered a human life that requires moral and legal protection. The question concerns what our judgment ought to be. To settle this issue, we must and do argue about our values and how they apply in this case.

Subjectivists might contend that even in questions on abortion, the arguments are still not about values but about facts, for example, facts concerning the consistency of our judgments. Our morality requires protection for infants. Perhaps, to be consistent, protection must also be granted to fetuses. But consistency in judgment is important only if we are talking about something over and above mere feelings or preferences. There is nothing wrong with desiring vanilla ice cream today and chocolate tomorrow. Morality does not work that way. Whatever militates against killing today also militates against killing tomorrow. Again, morality seems to involve much more than having and arousing feelings. Disagreements about what action is right may be difficult to resolve,[5] but we attempt to do so through rational argument — a point Ayer and Stevenson cannot capture.

The inference to be drawn from disagreements on moral issues is not that we cannot argue and discuss values, but that these are some of the most difficult discussions that human beings have. Our values, and the arguments about them, can lead in different directions. The abortion debate centers on conflicts between the value of freedom, in terms of the choices of the bearer, and the value of the life of the fetus. Both sides can agree that each value is important, but in the case of abortion, circumstances demand that one value must be deemed more important. The difficulty with this question is that there are strong points on both sides. Arguments grounded in freedom considerations are challenged by arguments grounded in considerations of human welfare. To say this is to emphasize that morality is not just a matter of personal belief or feeling, but also, and primarily, a matter of rational deliberation concerning the strength and importance of various considerations and values.

Still, Ayer and subjectivists in general are not likely to be convinced. At this point, they would raise their ultimate defense. Subjectivists fail to find any content to morality that would give each person sound reasons to adopt a similar moral outlook. Ayer discusses this position in terms of the impossibility of defining 'good.' For Ayer, if we cannot develop an objective definition of the central concept of morality, then morality can have no solid foundation. Each individual will be left to work out his or her own attitudes and feelings (no doubt with various influences from others) about what counts as good and, thus, about what counts as moral.

Many arguments are raised to show that there can be no definition of good. Suppose good is to be defined in terms of happiness. It is readily apparent that many acts that promote happiness are not good. It is inappropriate, for example, to promote happiness by stealing from others. Similar problems arise if good is defined in terms of freedom. It is unacceptable to respect freedom at the expense of the lives of others. The subjectivist would argue that no matter what definition of good is proposed, counterexamples can be raised to demonstrate that the definition is inadequate.

The subjectivist's flaw may be in oversimplifying the problem. The subjectivist seeks a single, brief statement of exactly what good means. Since we cannot substitute 'happiness' or 'freedom' or any such term or phrase for 'good' in all cases, there must be no objective definition of good and, thus, no solid foundation for morality.

The criticisms the subjectivist raised against defining good as happiness or freedom are no different from the objections raised in Chapter I to strict utilitarian and deontological accounts of moral considerations. For each proposed definition, counterexamples arise because some factors important for moral analysis are left out. Good cannot be defined as happiness because there are cases in which freedom can outweigh happiness. Far from indicating that morality is a matter of personal feeling, the counterexamples indicate the need to supplement one feature of moral goodness with others. This is, of course, exactly what was done in developing a complete account of moral considerations.

In short, the failure of attempts to define good prove not the subjectivity of morality but the complexity of morality. We cannot expect to find a simple definition that will apply in all cases and tell us quickly what action is right or wrong. Rather, we must understand the variety of moral considerations, determine which apply in particular cases, and, if conflicts arise, develop arguments that indicate which considerations are strongest and which act is right. Given the complexity of the entire process, it is no wonder that, on difficult moral problems, people can reach different conclusions. But they do so not simply because of different feelings, but because of different rational perspectives on the strengths of various moral considerations. Moral arguments are more than mere linguistic details or disputes over empirical fact. They are inquiries concerning how to act well and what is and ought to be important to human beings. Such a rational account of morality the subjectivist cannot explain.

2. Anthropological Defenses of Relativism

Unfortunately, it is one thing to say that individuals undertake moral analysis in a rational manner and quite another to say conclusively that morality is objective. Moral deliberations may involve rational analysis based on attitudes or beliefs that vary widely from society to society. Arguments that morality is essentially relative often make this claim. Each society works out, rationally and otherwise, a code for its members. But the code is grounded in the particular attitudes and beliefs of the culture. Since these starting points for social codes vary, so will the codes themselves. This diversity of moral codes then supports the claim that morality has shifting foundations.

No one can deny that there is a huge difference in moral judgments from community to community. It can be argued that if morality really were objective, we would be able to determine the right answer in cases of disagreement over proper actions. Since often we are not able to determine *the* morally right answer when different moral codes clash, morality must be relative to the beliefs and attitudes of particular communities.

Of course, sometimes firm conclusions can be drawn when judgments differ. Given the moral considerations of welfare and freedom, we can demonstrate that certain actions in other societies are morally wrong. Hitler's campaign to exterminate Jews and other people deemed undesirable represents the most obvious example. But this is an easy judgment to make — and it is not simply an external judgment. Many people in Germany during Hitler's regime would have considered the murder of innocent people to be morally wrong. That is why so many massacres occur out of the public eye.

The tough cases emerge when people in different communities make different judgments. Consider the following common cases in discussions of ethical relativity:

1. A society considers anyone from other societies to be a slave if the person is found in its territory. Members of this society consider their institution of slavery to be morally correct. Members of our society consider slavery to be wrong.

2. Members of a small island community routinely kill infants if a large number are born in a particular span of time. Members of this society consider infanticide morally acceptable.[6] Members of our society consider such actions to be wrong.

3. People in a community often help elderly family members commit suicide. Members of this society consider suicide and euthanasia morally acceptable. Members of our community do not.[7]

These are the types of cases cited by those developing an anthropological defense of the relativity of morality. On analysis, however, it is not at all clear that the examples do help to prove moral relativism.

In the slavery example, though judgments about slavery may differ depending on social orientation, it does not follow that the only relevant arguments depend on facts related to particular social backgrounds. The relativist must argue that in the slaveholding society, it is morally right to keep slaves, in the strong sense that there are no arguments that would provide moral reasons for people in such a society to give up slavery. The problem for the relativist is that while nothing about that particular culture may point against slavery, arguments that incorporate considerations relevant to people in general will still apply to the members of the slaveholding society. Considerations of welfare and freedom still militate against slavery.

Indeed, a member of the society that allowed slavery could understand and even make such arguments. Any progress toward the abolition of slavery is likely to result from individuals pressing arguments based on these considerations. This process was a major factor in the antislavery movement in the United States. But the arguments that took hold in the nineteenth century could have been made just as easily in earlier centuries. Indeed, many people in the sixteenth and seventeenth centuries did argue that slavery was immoral. Despite pressing moral arguments, societies can condone immoral practices. As Kellenberger notes, there is nothing in the fact that societies make different judgments that "rules out the possibility that some societies are mistaken in their moral beliefs."[8]

In the infanticide example, it might not be as clear that one side is right and the other wrong. Suppose, as might well be the case, that the island community lives at a subsistence level and lacks effective means of contraception and abortion. If children are born at a rate above the level that the community could support, something would have to be done. Either the community and everyone in it would be threatened or some individuals would have to be sacrificed. As Joseph Fletcher notes, "The world's finiteness is harder to hide on a Pacific coral reef."[9] Extra persons, in the form of newborn infants, would, unfortunately, be a reasonable group to sacrifice in order to maintain the lives of others.

In these situations, infanticide may be similar to killing in self-defense — just as we allow abortions in order to save the life of the bearer. To say that the island community practises infanticide may not imply that it performs what could clearly be called morally unacceptable actions. Rather, it is forced by circumstances to commit actions that in *other* situations would be wrong for all people. In this classic case, as in many others, it is highly misleading to say that one society considers an action wrong and another society considers it right. When circumstances are taken into account, the judgments may be quite compatible. At the least, each side may recognize the need for different judgments.

The reason for the apparent conflict is that the judgments are described in terms that are too simplistic. Where infanticide is accepted, it is not blanket acceptance. There is no general principle making it permissible to kill infants. Indeed, there is likely to be general abhorrence of infanticide. The disagreement across societies occurs over legitimate exceptions to a general obligation not to kill. As this obligation is applied to particular cases, the specific environmental situation will help to determine when killing is justified. A community leading a precarious existence may well face a number of situations in which it is necessary to kill to maintain the society. As the infanticide example indicates, cases in which different values seem to be present may really be cases in which changes in circumstances require different applications of the same values. Once again, differences at the level of specific applications, at stage three of moral analysis, need not imply the relativity of morality (of fundamental moral values).

In the euthanasia case, the situation may be even more complicated. In one version, the case can be the same as the infanticide example. A society may not be able to sustain all its members. As a result, the elderly who are unable to produce anymore might be willing to kill themselves or to allow themselves to die from the elements. Other persons may aid in such endeavors. Once again, circumstances require that some poeple die to save others in the community.

There is, however, another version of the euthanasia example. Suppose that a community can support its elderly but that as people become old, frail, and afflicted by various ailments, it is still common for them to decide — and to receive aid — to bring their lives to an end. In this case, circumstances do not make it necessary for people to die; something else motivates the decision.

In such a society, life itself is not always the dominant value. Issues about the quality of life can become more pressing. Peter Kolben describes the Hottentots' feelings concerning leaving elderly parents to starve in an isolated hut.

Is it not a cruelty . . . to suffer either man or woman to languish any considerable time under a heavy, motionless old age? Can you see a parent or relative shaking and freezing under a cold, dreary, heavy,

useless old age, and not think, in pity of them, of putting an end to
their misery by putting, which is the only means, an end to their old
days?[10]

To suffer through final years in pain, with reduced physical abilities,
without making contributions to the community or family, and drain-
ing resources that others could use more profitably, may be considered a worse wrong than bringing one's life to an end.

Here, to say that one society allows euthanasia while another
does not may mean that there is a fundamental disagreement about
values. One society places a stronger value and a more significant
obligation on continued physical existence, while another may put
greater emphasis on the type and quality of life that people will lead.

Even here, however, the difference is not about what counts as a
moral value but about how to weigh competing values. Each society
will value human life itself and the quality of that life. Each society
will develop features of its moral code that promote and protect both
values. The disagreement concerns which obligations are most important in specific clashes. Once again, the dispute emerges in terms of
the applications of action guides, and there may well be different but
equally acceptable answers. Good moral reasons may exist both for
choosing to end one's life when its quality sinks below a certain point
and for striving to continue one's physical existence until natural
causes end it.

This is a perfectly reasonable situation. Once the nature of moral
values and of basic moral considerations is clear, there will be many
situations in which obligations associated with the values will clash.
There will be clear cases in which one value will be more important,
and other cases in which the opposing value will be more important.
But there are also likely to be cases in which the values will be rather
well balanced. In these situations, it may be reasonable and morally
acceptable to decide either way. In each case, however, the underlying
values remain the same. Both sides accept the basic moral considerations, but work out the relationships among the resulting obligations
in slightly different ways. As long as the foundations remain the same,
argument between the sides can proceed, and it remains possible that
one side eventually will convince the other.

As a result, the original anthropological argument rests on a faulty assumption. For morality to be objective, it is not necessary that there be only one correct answer to moral problems. There are at least two senses in which different moral answers can be quite consistent with the objectivity of morality. First, the issue under discussion (e.g., infanticide) may really involve a number of different situations, each of which requires separate analysis and, perhaps, different answers. Changes in circumstances can yield alterations in moral judgments. Second, a single situation may (as in the euthanasia case) raise competing values in such a way that there is a close balance among the conflicting obligations. Here, it may be possible to develop good moral arguments for both sides. Communities or individuals will then be able to defend different but equally acceptable rankings of obligations. Morality remains a matter of developing a consistent, coherent, and rational position from objective moral considerations.

3. Objectivity, Morality, and the Hit-Man

The discussions of relativism and subjectivism have emphasized why moral analysis is a rational activity and the way in which different specific judgments can rationally emerge from common objective foundations. These conclusions dispute many popular accounts of relativism and subjectivism, for those accounts often search for moral objectivity at the wrong point. They search for objectivity at the final stage of moral analysis, at the level of applications of moral guides to specific cases. But decisions about specific actions are determined not just by moral values and considerations but by circumstances. Actions take place in the world, and the world has a significant effect on them and the general obligations that justify them. As previous discussion indicated, differences in circumstances can lead to differences in action. Here, the differences are the result of the relativity of situations, not the relativity of morality.

If the objectivity of morality is to be tested, it must be at a level that is not affected by facts about the particular situation. We must test morality's objectivity at the first stage in moral analysis, the basic moral considerations. It is not an accident that in examining various arguments in defense of subjectivism and relativism, the discussions always returned to the analysis of moral considerations.

In the examples cited, common foundations can be uncovered. The motivations for infanticide in the island community and euthanasia among the Hottentots are the same considerations that lead other communities (in different circumstances or because of different choices when values are balanced) to reject infanticide and euthanasia. It is consideration for the welfare of people in the community that leads islanders to kill infants when there is no other way to ensure the survival of any in the community, and it is respect for elderly parents and consideration for their welfare that lead the Hottentots to aid in ending the lives of the old, frail, and suffering. Though other cultures may not always agree with these specific actions, the objectivity of morality is assured if the foundations, the considerations that lead to rules and actions, are the same.

But subjectivists and relativists can extend their challenge. It is possible to contend that individuals or societies need not accept considerations of welfare and freedom as appropriate foundations for moral deliberations. Certainly, some individuals (e.g., hardened criminals with no concern for their victims) and groups (e.g., organized criminal bands concerned only for their own gain) reject these values. The existence of such individuals and organizations can lead to a reemergence of relativism and subjectivism at the first stage of moral analysis: it is just a matter of individual feeling or social attitude whether to accept considerations of human welfare and freedom as basic moral considerations.

There is some truth in this claim. Individuals must accept the importance of moral considerations. Unlike the need for food, a commitment to morality does not automatically emerge in people. As a result, there will be some people who do not make the commitment to morality. Our initial reaction to such people may be to argue with them, to show them that they are wrong. But with people who feel that considerations of human welfare and freedom are not relevant to their actions, it is not clear what can be said.

If we tried to convince a hit-man that considerations of welfare and freedom militate against earning a living as a hired killer, the outcome is likely to be unsatisfying.[11] The hit-man could claim that for him, human welfare and freedom do not represent relevant considerations at all. He is only concerned with his personal well-being. In a sense, this is the problem that Ayer was raising when he contended that if there is real disagreement over values — i.e., over what counts as a moral consideration — further argument is pointless; we have no choice but to accept the differences. The hit-man would reject as irrelevant any moral reasons presented against murder. Relativists and subjectivists might take this as further evidence that even the foundations of morality are just a matter of individual or social attitude.

But the fact that people or societies will believe and act immorally need not threaten the objectivity of morality any more than the fact that some people add incorrectly threatens the existence of objective principles of mathematics. This point can be explained in terms of a distinction between:

1. Factors accepted as relevant — Included here will be whatever does motivate the judgments of an individual or a community. For some people, like the hit-man, these factors will be limited to self-interested considerations.

2. Objective considerations — Included here will be those factors for which good reasons, based on features independent of personal or social attitudes, can be raised for including them in deliberations.[12]

In other words, something can *be* a consideration even if it is not *accepted* as a consideration. While it may be impossible to convince the hit-man of the objectivity and importance of considerations of welfare and freedom, it may still be reasonable to contend that morality does, indeed, have objective foundations. Particular individuals may accept many points for which they have inadequate reasons and may reject many points for which there are very good reasons. The fact that some people reject a point that has solid support does not imply that the point is incorrect or poorly grounded.

The predicament with the hit-man is analogous to the situation concerning the International Flat Earth Research Society.[13] The group is composed of individuals who believe that the earth truly is flat, that there is no gravity, and that the sun and moon are thirty-two-mile-wide balls floating three thousand miles above the earth. Members of the society are familiar with the course of Western science and the evidence amassed to prove that the earth is a ball orbiting the sun.

They, like the hit-man in the moral arena, reject all arguments presented by their opposition. They consider pictures of the earth from space to be faked and space flights and lunar landings to be staged by NASA.

We do not consider the existence of people who believe that the world is flat to shake our belief that the world is spherical. We are still convinced by the evidence that members of the Flat Earth Society try to ignore. The same situation can obtain concerning our reaction to those who do not accept welfare and freedom considerations.

To determine whether the earth is a sphere or whether there are good reasons to accept freedom and welfare considerations as objective foundations for morality, we must look not to who or how many people believe the point but to whether the relevant evidence is sufficient to prove the point. The issue concerning the objectivity of morality centers on whether foundations for moral analysis that are relevant to all people can be found. Considerations of welfare and freedom, since they are derived from features of human nature, apply to human beings as a species. No matter what an individual's particular religious or cultural background, the considerations apply to his or her existence. As a result, the relevance of these features is independent of individual feelings or social attitudes.

We must look to facts about persons and not what specific people believe. Bonnie Steinbock notes, "You ought not to stick pins in Lionel, for example, because doing this hurts him. We would not withdraw this judgment upon learning that you are perfectly indifferent to his suffering. It is this suffering that gives you a reason to stop, and that reason seems to be independent of how you feel about it."[14] Steinbock explains the pressing nature of Lionel's suffering in terms of a recognition of the reality of other people. Whether or not someone does accept the existence of human suffering, it is there and can provide a reason for avoiding harm to others.

The discussion has returned once again to questions about human nature and the considerations that arise from human talents, needs, and desires. Because humans are beings of a specific and readily explained type, the welfare and freedom of such beings emerge as moral values and, thus, as foundations for moral analysis. Since these considerations are based on features and capacities common to the human species, there is nothing involved that can be relative to particular individuals or communities. The values associated with welfare and freedom apply universally to human beings. As Kluckholn notes, "Psychology, psychiatry, sociology, and anthropology in different ways and on somewhat different evidence converge in attesting to similar human needs and psychic mechanisms."[15] These similarities indicate the respects in which the foundations for moral codes converge. Though circumstances and rankings of values may yield different rules of action, it is possible to understand and, in many instances, to accept the divergent views as legitimate moral perspectives.

4. Conclusion

It is important not to let the fact that individuals and cultures differ on moral issues blind us to the objective arguments that can be provided in support of the foundations for morality. Some differences (as with the slaveholding society) will be morally indefensible, but others (as in the euthanasia and infanticide cases) may be justified and explained within an objective framework provided by the basic considerations of welfare and freedom. When one examines the heart of morality, that level unaffected by extraneous factors, it is possible to explain the solid foundations for moral analysis — even if some persons reject those arguments. In Chapter I, those basic considerations were uncovered. Here, the strength of those considerations as a foundation for morality has been explained. We are now able to build on the foundations.

Notes

1. A.J. Ayer, *Language, Truth, and Logic* (New York: Dover Publications, Inc., 1952); see especially the Introduction and Chapter 6.

2. C.L. Stevenson's view is developed in *Facts and Values* (New Haven, CT: Yale University Press, 1963) and *Ethics and Language* (New Haven, CT: Yale University Press, 1944). Citations below are from "The Emotive Meaning of Ethical Terms," in *Facts and Values*, pp. 10–31.

3. Ayer, p. 107.

4. Stevenson, p. 16.

5. This should not mask the fact that, in many cases, differences *are* resolved.

6. Robert Louis Stevenson's famous account of Polynesian communities that practice infanticide has made this example a popular one.

7. Kellenberger explains and analyzes such cases in detail. See J. Kellenberger, "Ethical Relativism," *Journal of Value Inquiry*, Vol. 13 (Spring 1979), especially pp. 12–13.

8. Kellenberger, p. 10.

9. Joseph Fletcher, "The Ethics of Genetic Control," in *Contemporary Issues in Bioethics*, eds. Tom L. Beauchamp and LeRoy Walters (Belmont, CA: Wadsworth Publishing Co., 1978), p. 585.

10. Peter Kolben, *Present State of the Cape of Good Hope* (1731: London), p. 319, cited by Karl Dunker, "Ethical Relativity? (An Enquiry into the Psychology of Ethics)," in *Ethical Relativity*, ed. John Ladd (Belmont, CA: Belmont Publishing Co., 1973), p. 46. In some respects, this example is influenced by circumstances. Our culture is better able to care for the elderly — at least in terms of eliminating visible discomforts. That there is more to the case is evident, however, from the fact that some cultures would refuse to end the life of an elderly parent even if that life were as painful as that described by the Hottentots.

11. The hit-man example is borrowed from Gilbert Harman's important philosophical defense of relativism. Harman's view is developed in "Moral Relativism Defended," *Philosophical Review*, 84 (1975), pp. 3–22; "Relativistic Ethics: Morality as Politics," *Midwest Studies in Philosophy*, 3 (1978), pp. 109–21; and *The Nature of Morality* (New York: Oxford University Press, 1977).

12. This distinction is based on B.C. Postow's distinction between (1) being a reason and (2) being accepted as a reason. The former would involve what could appropriately motivate action, even if it did not, because it lacked acceptance. (B.C. Postow, "Moral Relativism Avoided," *Personalist* Vol. 60 [January 1979], pp. 95–100.)

13. See David Gates and Jennifer Smith, "Keeping the Flat-Earth Faith," *Newsweek*, July 2, 1984, p. 12.

14. Bonnie Steinbock, "Moral Reasons and Relativity," *Journal of Value Inquiry*, Vol. 15 (1981), p. 165.

15. Clyde Kluckholn, "Ethical Relativism: *Sic et Non*," in *Ethical Relativism*, ed. John Ladd, p. 90.

Stage Two:

General Obligations as Action Guides

Chapter III

Universal and Special Moral Obligations

I t is now necessary to move to the second stage of moral analysis, the elaboration of guides to action. These guides represent standards that are or ought to be appealed to in deliberations about specific actions. Clearly, there can be many types of guides: moral, religious, and legal, to name a few. This chapter will discuss the nature of moral action guides, which I will describe loosely as moral obligations. Chapter IV will examine the relationships between moral guides and other types.

In the moral realm, action guides serve as a bridge between what is valued — the basic moral considerations — and specific judgments about particular actions. These guides can be described as presumptions: the actions explained by the guides are *expected* or *presumed* to be followed unless there are sufficient counterreasons; that is, unless other guides are more important in a particular case. The simple rule "Do not lie!" represents a guide that is expected to be followed unless, for example, the lie is necessary to mislead an attacker pursuing an innocent victim. Thus, a statement of the guide alone is not enough to determine what persons should do in specific situations. It is also necessary to relate the guide to the particular case. But this task moves us to the third stage of moral analysis. Before we get there, we need to examine the guides themselves.

The fundamental role of moral guides is to provide us with some general, easily understood accounts of what morality demands. Basic moral considerations can be formulated into guides to action by explaining, for general types of situations, what respect for the considerations involves. An important way respect for human life is explicated is through a rule against killing. Another way is through a rule to render aid in life-threatening emergencies. The guides represent a way of formulating the values associated with moral considerations into rules for action or modes of behavior.

All moral action guides express in some way the obligations that are encumbent on human beings as moral agents. These obligations can be described in a variety of ways:

1. The most general and obvious type are rules or principles. These are statements that are often expressed as explicit commands: "Do this!" or "Don't do that!"

2. Virtues represent a second, less explicit type of guide. These describe traits or habits that characterize a good person. A just person is one who is disposed to act justly in specific situations. Virtues are not explicit statements about how to act; rather they represent general modes of behavior.

3. Rights constitute a third type of action guide. These are especially important guides, expressed in terms of what persons are owed by others.

The three ways of expressing moral guides or obligations do not yield opposing demands on individuals. To be virtuous means that one will perform actions consistent with the demands of explicit rules or principles. To respect someone's right to life requires following rules such as "Do not kill!" It is important, however, not just to know the rules but also (1) to be the type of person who is moved by the considerations underlying the rules, that is, to be virtuous, and (2) to understand which rules are associated with the particularly important demands associated with rights. Given their special characters, rights and virtues will be explained in some detail in later chapters.[1] In this chapter, I will examine moral action guides in general, without particular emphasis on the various ways those obligations can be expressed.

1. Two Types of Moral Obligations

It is important to remember that many common moral obligations gain support from both welfare and freedom considerations. In most cases, there are good utilitarian and deontological reasons against killing, stealing, or lying. Such actions not only threaten people's welfare but also limit or interfere with their decision-making abilities. As noted in Chapter I, lying can interfere with an individual's freedom to choose because it prevents the person from making a decision based on proper information. Lying can also lead to welfare harms, since a bad decision can affect well-being.

Since moral considerations were derived from factors common to human beings as a species, there is no basis for distinctions among types of humans in terms of the applicability of moral obligations. The life or health of a male, female, young or old person carries the same weight in moral decision-making. In addition, the rational choices of a male, female, young or old person ought to be respected equally. An important sense of human equality emerges here. Individuals must take account of the freedom and welfare of every individual affected by his or her actions. In moral deliberations, no one's interests can be forgotten because the deliberator simply does not care for the individual. Aversion may be grounds for avoiding dinner dates with someone, but it is not acceptable grounds for disregarding the implications of one's actions on the individual's life or ability to carry out personal goals. Since moral considerations represent factors that are essential to a human existence, it cannot be left to individuals to decide which persons ought to be granted moral consideration.

Two issues emerge here. We ask not only to whom moral obligations extend but also who must deal with moral obligations in decision-making. All humans must — in so far as they are able — take account of moral obligations. Though this statement may sound obvious, it needs elaboration. While many obligations associated with moral action guides are encumbent on all persons, it is possible for individuals to gain additional and special obligations.

Most moral philosophers have dealt primarily with how individuals, considered simply as persons, ought to treat others. Bentham's principle of utility and Kant's universal rules are expected (1) to apply to everyone equally and (2) to be followed by everyone. No one has a license to act immorally. Each one of us, no matter what income level, role, status, or race, is able to interfere with or threaten the lives, happiness, and freedom of others. Thus, people must always keep in mind the moral obligations that arise from considerations of human welfare and individual freedom. Those obligations arising from the moral considerations applied by people in general I will call *universal obligations*.

On the other hand, some moral obligations apply primarily to specific individuals. Guides that must be applied by individuals because of particular features of their situation I will speak of as *special* or *role obligations*. Each of us has a number of roles, as a student, parent, club member, or friend. Many of these positions delineate activities that people have decided to work into their lives. Thus, individuals voluntarily accept obligations that result, for example, from joining a club or profession. Special obligations can, however, be thrust upon people. Individuals sometimes become parents when they do not want to, and in times of national crisis, individuals can be drafted into military service. The discussions in this chapter will focus on special obligations that are a result of personal choice, though much of what is said will apply to nonvoluntary special moral obligations.

Indeed, often there is not a sharp dividing line between voluntarily accepted special obligations and those thrust upon people. Military draftees may be the clearest case of nonvoluntary role obligations, but even here there can be some voluntary aspects to the role. Many draftees feel a commitment to their country and some willingness to protect it. Though they would not go so far as to volunteer for duty, if a draft notice comes, many — though certainly not all — would view it not simply as a choice between army or jail but as an opportunity to fulfill a duty to their country. In these cases, the draft notice may be more like a gentle prod than a gun at the back.

On the other extreme, the decision to enter a profession such as law may seem to yield purely voluntary special obligations. There is no threat associated with the decision to become a lawyer, and there is no necessity to choose this occupation. There can, however, be pressure to enter a particular field — pressure from family or from oneself. Further, once an individual decides to become a lawyer, fulfillment of the special obligations of the profession is required; failure to do so can bring sanctions. Thus, at times, even voluntarily accepted special obligations can appear as threats.

As a result, it is more important to examine the nature of special moral obligations and their relationships to universal moral obligations than to dwell on the ways special obligations arise. Consider the mundane case of club membership. Being a member of a club may mean no more than deciding whether to attend meetings once a month. It is easy, however, for moral considerations and resulting special obligations to accompany this role. If you are a member of a bridge club and will be one of only four members to meet on a certain day, the fact that others will not be able to play properly without you is something to consider when deciding whether to attend. Because you have taken on a specific role as a club member, you must consider the welfare and happiness of other members in special ways. Of course, this does not mean that in every case you must attend. Other factors, such as providing aid to accident victims, might be more pressing in specific situations. The essential point is that nonmembers need not take account of the difficulties to arise from the meeting being short one player in the same way that members must.

Special moral obligations emerge when one has undertaken a role the performance of which other persons count on (or can be expected to count on) when they decide how to act. As long as it does not matter to anyone whether one attends a club meeting, there is no special moral obligation. As soon as others legitimately count on one's attendance, moral considerations are relevant in additional ways, and role obligations emerge.

Role obligations, then, exist alongside universal ones:

Stage 1: *Foundations*	*Moral Considerations* Factors, based on a concern for human beings in general, that must be taken into account in decision-making	
	Applied by persons in general Factors that everyone ought to consider	*Applied by persons in special circumstances* Factors that certain individuals ought to consider
	(yield)	(yield)
Stage 2: *Action Guides*	*Universal* *Obligations*	*Special or Role* *Obligations*

A fundamental point is highlighted by the above chart. Special moral obligations do not yield new values. What must be considered — that is, features associated with human welfare and freedom — remains the same. The distinction between special and universal obligations concerns the range of application, the specific ways individuals must take account of moral considerations. Universal obligations point out the ways individuals simply as persons must deal with moral considerations; special obligations delineate respects in which specific roles provide new ways the original considerations of welfare and freedom must be accounted for.

2. Examples of Special Moral Obligations

It is important to note the variety of special moral obligations. Consider two common situations in which such duties arise: parenting and promising. With respect to parenting, people undertake a wide variety of obligations with respect to particular individuals, that is, their own children. Once one becomes a parent, one must consider the needs of another being in ways unnecessary with respect to any other individuals. Parents must provide for the physical, emotional, and educational requirements of children. To take such control over others (even other children) would generally represent inappropriate interference; not to do so with respect to one's own children would be neglect. Because of the special relationship between parent and child, the moral considerations of welfare and freedom carry significantly more weight, and this means that more of one's life must be devoted to the welfare and freedom of others when those others are one's offspring.

In the case of parenting, a wide range of considerations and obligations arises concerning a limited number of individuals. Promising, on the other hand, is a social arrangement that enables an individual to generate generally limited special obligations with respect to any number of other people. Though usually rather specific, a promise can concern anything, from an agreement to meet for lunch at a certain time to a commitment to provide money for medical expenses. Promises can be jointly undertaken (each of us promises to help the other) or one-sided (I promise to help you) or third-party (I promise Joe to help you). In each case, the promisor places himself or herself under a new obligation to the promisee — and accepts new considerations on deliberations. To have promised is to have committed oneself to benefitting another in special ways. By not fulfilling the promise, one can also harm the promisee in special ways. Making a promise and breaking it is likely to hurt another much more significantly than not performing the same action when no promise was made.

Many special moral obligations emerge with respect to occupational roles. Every employee has role obligations to the employer and to fellow workers. Accepting a job yields a committment similar to that associated with joint promising. The employer agrees to provide pay and benefits for work the employee agrees to perform. The employer's interests and those of fellow workers can be harmed because actions they legitimately counted on were not performed. Many persons have argued that employees also owe their employer confidentiality and loyalty.[2] These represent further ways individuals in the role of employee must take special account of the interests of the employer. Significant moral problems can arise when obligations to the employer conflict with obligations as a person; for example, when one's company is seriously and surreptitiously polluting the air.

Managers and executives of publicly owned corporations have a variety of special obligations. There are role obligations relating to other employees, to stockholders, and even to the community as a whole. The common perception of people in a capitalistic system as actively pursuing only their own good is very misleading. While the ultimate goal of many economic activities may be personal gain, this is accomplished by operating in a complex network of reciprocal obligations. Even the corporate officer is paid *for achieving the good of the company.*

Professions such as medicine and law have long dealt with questions of role obligations. These occupations serve primarily a service function. The basic goal of the medical profession is to promote people's health; lawyers exist to serve a vital function in the judicial system. As a result, the medical and legal professions have developed codes of ethics to underline the considerations and obligations associated with these occupations. Western medical codes arose with the ancient Greeks. The Hippocratic Oath is primarily a code of ethics; each physician vows to "come [to a home] for the benefit of the sick" and never to "give a deadly drug." Current codes have, of course, retained the emphasis on the physician's role as a healer. In part to promote healing, contemporary medical codes have also emphasized the confidentiality of information about patients and the importance of the patient's understanding and consent with regard to treatment.

Lawyers, as might be expected, have developed a long and complicated code of ethics. Still, the basic principles are what one would expect. The advocate's dual function as an officer of the court and as a representative of a client is recognized. Thus, in the Code of Professional Responsibility for lawyers, one can find general canons asserting that (1) a lawyer should represent a client zealously within the bounds of the law (in criminal proceedings, defense attorneys must be zealous whether or not the client committed the crime), and (2) a lawyer should assist in improving the legal system (without regard to the interests of clients).[3] The code is, in essence, a statement of the requirements and ideals imposed on lawyers as individuals who have accepted a crucial role in the system of justice.

As many of the above examples indicate, special moral obligations are usually accorded to specific individuals. A parent is obligated to *his or her* children. Physicians and lawyers have special obligations to *their particular* patients and clients. But people in particular roles have obligations to *any* individual who enters the appropriate relationship. Parents cannot (morally) decide to help one child but not another; lawyers cannot aid one client but not a second. This is similar to the sense in which universal moral obligations apply to human beings equally: as a person, one must take account of the welfare and freedom of any individual who might be affected by one's actions. One's children or clients, however, can be especially affected by one's actions.

To make a promise or to enter a certain profession and, thus, to accept certain special moral obligations is not to absolve oneself of obligations as a person. And, of course, moral problems can arise when universal moral obligations clash with special ones. To understand the nature of such conflicts, it is necessary to develop a more systematic account of special moral obligations and their relationships to universal ones.

3. A Philosophical Account of Role Obligations

F.H. Bradley is one philosopher who has emphasized the importance of role obligations in moral thinking. He describes his theory as "my station and its duties," which clearly invokes the obligations that arise from one's position. In Bradley's terms, "the demand for a code of right in itself, apart from any stage, is seen to be the asking for an impossibility."[4]

The stage Bradley speaks of will be defined by the roles people play in various social organizations from family to nation. One's station is not simple. Each person has a variety of special roles, based on occupation, family setting, citizenship, place in society, and personal interests. The totality of these roles, which represent a person's unique station, defines the individual. For example, it is only as a mother, sister, corporate executive, American, Illinoisan, Democrat, and sailor that an individual has any identity. As Bradley notes, "We have found ourselves when we have found our station and its duties, our function as an organ in the social organism."[5] Bradley obviously emphasizes that humans are social beings; there is no individual (beyond a mere physical animal) except through social development and relationships.

"What [the individual] has to do depends on what his place is, what his function is, and that all comes from his station in the organism."[6] To decide how to act, people must look to their particular position in the community. But though any role can generate special demands, it does not follow that every role will yield special *moral obligations*. A role in a criminal organization as a hit-man hardly generates a special moral obligation to kill. Organizations can embody immoral goals and, thus, yield immoral roles. It is essential to determine when roles are morally acceptable and generate special moral obligations.

Bradley is aware of the need to discover some method for determining the appropriateness of various roles and the responsibilities they engender. He argues that we must view the variety of roles individuals undertake as subsumed under and legitimized by a single central role: the role as a member of a nation or, in Bradley's terms, a state. The national state unifies roles and sets the tone for people's existence.

> We must say that a man's life with its moral duties is in the main filled up by his station in that system of wholes which the state is, and that

this, partly by its laws and institutions and still more by its spirit, gives him the life which he does live and ought to live.[7]

It is the state, conceived broadly as both the political establishment and the national culture, that is responsible for providing the individual with a language, a way of thinking, and a set of basic values. While it would be possible for individuals to give up many roles (for example, political party affiliations and occupations), it would be almost impossible to alter or to give up one's nationality in the sense Bradley speaks of. People may move to a different country and change their citizenship, but they will, for a long period, retain the cultural heritage of their original homeland. We see this phenomenon often in the United States. People move here from all parts of the world and bring with them, and reestablish here, many of the traditions of their native lands. Bradley would explain this in terms of the major influence a person's original culture has in molding the individual.

Further, it is within a national culture that other roles arise and are sanctioned. In our society, the role of parent is defined in part by the needs and beliefs of the community, and is even enforced through legal mechanisms which demand a certain level of care for children. Occupational roles are also influenced by legal and cultural factors. Businesspeople in our free enterprise society have very different roles from managers of planned economies. The search for personal profits, so appropriate in our economy, would be disdained in the Soviet system. On the other hand, a national culture can determine that certain roles are unacceptable — and that performing them can be immoral. A role in a criminal organization is just such an unacceptable position.

Bradley's analysis yields a crucial point. Roles and the resulting responsibilities do not exist in isolation. What is demanded by special moral obligations arises out of particular roles, but the obligations will be justified as morally appropriate with reference to a wider context. For Bradley, they are part of an interconnected whole that is unified by the central role as a member of a state. As he might say, fulfilling the obligations associated with the role of a physician is morally appropriate because that role is sanctioned by and is important to the healthy functioning of the state.

Bradley's account, however, may need further development. His reliance on the state issues from his belief in the importance of the state in each person's development. The central role of the nation in the lives of its members cannot be denied. There is no international community that helps to define individuals in a concrete way. Relations among people from different nations are often defined by the customs and statutes of the home nations of the participants. But the issue of how individuals come to be what they are is very different from that of how to explain and to justify the specific roles and responsibilities individuals have.

The basic question emerges again. The state may well be central to the individual's existence; other roles may be sanctioned and defined by the laws and traditions of the state. But what makes the state and its laws and customs morally acceptable? Bradley admits that states are never perfect, that they are, in essence, constantly evolving toward a higher moral plane. But he still contends that people must look to the state at its current stage of evolution as the central organism from which roles and role obligations flow. Perhaps in Bradley's home, Great Britain, with its history of progress on human rights and improvements in welfare for its citizens, we could leave the state such a crucial role in determining what morality demands. Other states seem to be less reliable. The rise of the Nazis in Germany may indicate that nations can change far too quickly on moral issues to be left as the keepers of the moral torch.

Bradley recognizes the problem here. He admits that ultimately morality cannot be taken simply from the community one is in. Even the best community will have defects. It is important to be able to judge the moral acceptability of the state as well as of the various organizations and roles within the state. As a result, a good person will reflect on the morality of his or her state and will attempt to make it better, that is, more consistent with a universal morality not linked to any particular time or country. Bradley notes that there can be an ideal of a good person who "is not good as a member of this or that community, but who realizes himself in whatever community he finds himself."[8] It is generally just such a universal morality that is used to judge the actual moralities of particular groups, families, professions, and nations.

If we want to justify roles and their resulting responsibilities, we must look to the foundations for any moral obligations. Though special obligations will arise and be *explained* in terms of the roles that an individual occupies, those obligations will be *sanctioned* as moral obligations only in so far as they are based on considerations of human welfare and freedom. These considerations serve to distinguish role obligations of parents from those of hit-men. The former are designed to aid individuals and people in general by providing care for those not yet able to care for themselves — and thus ensuring the functioning of the community in the future. The hit-man, on the other hand, is concerned only with the well-being of certain individuals. More importantly, he accomplishes this by causing serious harms to others and, thus, by ignoring considerations of human welfare and freedom as they relate to the victims. The national goal of the Nazis can be criticized on similar grounds.

Special moral obligations are justified, then, not simply by the state but by the basic moral considerations that provide the foundation for any moral action guides. Once again, we see that the difference between universal and special obligations concerns not their justification but their range of applicability. Universal obligations explain guides for any person's actions, regardless of that person's nationality, occupation, or other specific roles or characteristics. Special moral obligations represent guides for individuals in so far as they occupy specific roles. These roles may arise and be explained with reference to a national culture and legal system, but the obligations associated with roles will be moral ones only if they are based on the basic moral considerations of human welfare and freedom.

4. *Relationships between Universal and Special Obligations*

The discussion of Bradley's philosophy highlights the common foundation of both universal and special moral obligations. There is no doubt that special roles can lead to moral obligations that are encumbent only on persons in those roles. But there remain the obligations that concern people simply as people. Some of the most difficult moral dilemmas involve clashes of universal and special obligations. It becomes important, then, to see how these two types of moral obligations relate.

Special moral obligations often reinforce universal ones. The physician has a stronger obligation to aid his or her patients in need than do the rest of us. Health professionals must provide aid for accident victims whether they are patients or not. Ordinary persons certainly have obligations to get aid, but this requires significantly less than what is demanded of physicians. Similarly, lawyers have a much stronger obligation to protect their clients' rights. Those not associated with the legal profession need only avoid interference in people's legal rights; lawyers must take positive steps to ensure and to utilize such rights.

Often, no serious problems arise here. The additional responsibilities are quite consistent with universal moral duties. Obligations simply as a person leave much space for further, special responsibilities. In providing medical services, the physician usually does not have to choose between acting on special obligations or universal ones.[9]

This is the most common relationship between universal and special moral obligations. Role obligations simply add new demands or strengthen old ones without in any way weakening or conflicting with existing universal obligations. This situation is analogous to adding one more meeting to a day's schedule. Usually this does not mean one must miss an existing meeting. Generally, there is time to fit in another session.

But new meetings or new role obligations can yield conflicts. Consider the case of a physician with a patient who needs surgery to survive but who will not agree to it. The physician can be torn between an obligation as a health professional to heal when possible and an obligation as a person not to coerce others. To be sure, there are cases in which the patient is irrational and is not capable of making a decision. Here, the physician or family members may have to decide. Often, however, the recalcitrant patient is not incompetent. After all, there are always risks associated with surgery, and it need not be irrational — though it may be a bad decision — to avoid those risks and to take whatever time one has left. These situations are not unknown in medical settings, and physicians, nurses, hospital administrators, judges, and juries have had to deal with the question of whether role obligations or universal obligations are most pressing. (Related problems emerge with other roles. Corporate executives often have to decide whether to uphold a general obligation to the community, e.g., in terms of avoiding pollution, as opposed to a special obligation to stockholders, e.g., to return profits to them.)

For people not in the physician's role, the conflict described above need not be a serious dilemma. It is inappropriate for people in general to force or to dupe someone into undergoing an operation. But special moral obligations can alter the way moral considerations are ranked. The physician's special duty to heal may justify some misrepresentation in order to convince a patient to accept necessary surgery.

Benjamin Freedman has explained this phenomenon with reference to medical confidentiality. Freedman notes that medical confidentiality is a stronger requirement than the ordinary (universal) obligation not to disclose personal information about others. "A reason which might suffice to justify divulging a friend's secret — say, "it's best for all concerned" — would not suffice for a physician to disclose medical information."[10] In other words, in situations where it may be *right* for a friend to divulge a secret, it would still be *wrong* for a physician to divulge confidential medical information.[11]

The reason for this strong emphasis on confidentiality in medicine is that the primary goal of the profession would be impossible — or, at least, extremely hard — to achieve without it. In their roles as health professionals, physicians are motivated by one primary ideal, based on the goal of the profession to heal. In deliberations, added weight is given this central consideration. "[This] value is basic in professional morality, whereas in ordinary morality it is one among many others."[12] As a result, corollaries of the central value, that is, factors that are essential for achieving the goal, are also given added weight. Physicians cannot heal effectively if people will not provide facts about their illnesses, and people are not likely to supply such information if they think it may become cocktail-party conversation. This provides the basis for the extra strength accorded medical confidentiality.

The difference between ordinary and medical confidentiality arises with respect to exceptions to the rule. Medical confidentiality allows fewer exceptions than ordinary confidentiality. What follows is that in the vast majority of cases, in which there is no question about exceptions, medical and ordinary confidentiality demand the same thing, namely, that personal information not be disclosed. In addition, in those cases in which reasons are sufficient to override medical confidentiality, ordinary confidentiality would also be overridden. The only differences occur in those relatively few cases in which ordinary confidentiality would be overridden and medical confidentiality would not.

It is, of course, when special and universal obligations yield different results that decision-making is most difficult. A number of such cases arise with respect to confidentiality. Consider the case of a psychiatric patient who expresses an interest in harming or stealing from someone. Here, universal obligations for the intended victim clash with the psychiatrist's special obligation to the patient. As Freedman notes, the special obligations may lead to a decision contrary to what would be generally expected. The obligation of ordinary persons to keep personal information private would be outweighed by the obligation to avoid harms to others. A psychiatrist, on the other hand, can only provide medical services if people are willing to divulge their innermost feelings, desires, and plans. Even information about certain crimes may have to be kept confidential in order to preserve the effectiveness of the profession. Thus, the added weight accorded some values by special moral obligations yields a different decision about what counts as morally correct action.

Similar alterations in the ordering of considerations occur in other professions. Medical confidentiality has a direct analogue in the legal profession. Lawyers also have a strong obligation not to divulge information provided by clients. The reason for such a requirement is similar to that for medical confidentiality. The legal profession cannot perform its function in a system of justice unless its clients are willing to provide their lawyers with appropriate information.

In these cases, special obligations still provide only a different ranking of moral obligations. Freedman explains that the central goal of the medical profession "is not an evil wish, a desire to be wicked. It is, rather, an exaggerated emphasis upon one [moral] ideal to the detriment of some others, the zealous embracing of one value with which they are professionally identified."[13] As noted above, special moral obligations do not generate new values; the basic consideration of human welfare remains at the heart of medical values. But having a special obligation may tip the scales in favor of one moral demand as opposed to another that would be the more pressing in ordinary settings.

Special moral obligations can sometimes alter ethical decision-making in even more significant ways. Consider the example of a lawyer whose client is charged with murder — a murder the client did in fact commit. The lawyer knows this, but because of the insufficient evidence amassed by the prosecution, a good defense will lead to an innocent verdict. The attorney, acting on his or her special obligation as a defense counsel, provides the best service possible, and the murderer is set free.

This situation differs from the medical example above. Medical confidentiality represents an exaggerated emphasis on an obligation that all people share. Physicians must take greater pains to uphold confidentiality, even if that sometimes means placing less emphasis on other obligations. On the other hand, the lawyer's special obligation to defend clients independently of whether they committed the crime generates new responsibilities that can, in specific contexts, erase some universal obligations. The lawyer's attempt to avoid the conviction of a client would almost always be wrong if performed in anything but the defense attorney's role. Since the legal system is the means used to identify and to protect ourselves against people who threaten the community, individuals in general have a moral (as well as a legal) obligation to aid in convicting persons whose immoral actions also violate the law. It is wrong to help someone who has committed a murder to escape appropriate legal punishment. But the defense attorney is required to do just that; the attorney acts improperly if anything less is done.

Related situations can also be found in medical settings. Persons often speak of physicians "playing god." In an important sense, however, such cases can also be described as "playing the devil." When physicians must decide who will get a scarce medical resource or when to take a comatose patient off life-support systems, the agonizing aspect of the decision arises because someone will die. It is generally impermissible for individuals to decide that another person will die, but physicians are sometimes placed in a position of having to do just that.

In these cases, the special obligations are not just a matter of exaggerating existing universal obligations. Rather, the roles generate new and different obligations. The defense attorney has a duty to provide legal services independently of whether the client committed the deed in question. The physician has a duty to determine who is to receive scarce medical services. In both situations, these additional obligations can directly conflict with existing universal guides.

Both the physician allocating scarce medical resources and the lawyer defending a guilty client are forced to seriously consider actions that would be impermissible for persons in general. The lawyer's predicament seems to be a variation of what Michael Walzer calls the problem of "dirty hands." Walzer explains this situation with respect to the actions of politicians. He describes the difficulties in gaining and keeping power, the crooked deals, the exaggerated promises, the outright lies, and the broken promises that are part of governing. In so far as such actions are sometimes necessary in political life, politicians will sometimes act in immoral ways.[14] The paradox is that we want good people (those who are interested in governing for the benefit of the community) to do the wrongs. In detailing the plight of a good candidate whose election depends on making a deal with a dishonest ward boss, Walzer notes, "It is important to stress that we don't want just anyone to make the deal; we want him to make it, precisely because he has scruples about it. . . . If he is the good man I am imagining him to be, he will feel guilty, that is, he will believe himself to be guilty. That is what it means to have dirty hands. . . . "[15]

Walzer's willingness to live with a significant amount of immorality on the part of political leaders is controversial. His analysis does, however, help to explain the example of the lawyer who successfully defends a guilty client. In both cases, an act that would normally be completely wrong is performed with some moral support. The politician can be elected and can govern well only by making the deal; the lawyer can uphold the system of justice only by performing his or her role as well as possible.

In both cases, it is a special obligation associated with a particular role that makes the action at all appropriate. The individual actors are not functioning alone; they are part of a process whose success depends on a number of persons fulfilling separate tasks. It is the importance of (1) the ultimate goal, with its significant moral backing, and (2) the individual's role, as one piece of the process to achieve the goal, that can lead to actions that simply deny universal moral obligations.

The case in defense of the lawyer's actions, however, seems significantly stronger than that for the politician's. Indeed, judgments of the actors are likely to be quite different. The lawyer, in aiding the criminal, will be said to have acted rightly, though the results may be unfortunate. The politician, on the other hand, may well be judged to have acted wrongly in making the deal, even though the ultimate goal was appropriate. As Walzer explains, if possible, "we would honor him for the good he has done, and we would punish him for the bad he has done."[16]

Perhaps the reason for the difference in judgment relates to the degree of closeness between the specific action and the obligations associated with the role. The system of justice is directly threatened if defense attorneys do not perform their role in protecting the legal rights of the client. It is difficult to blame or to punish someone who performs a function that is essential to the proper operation of such an important social institution. The importance of the role and the system in which the role is played makes the attorney's action right.

The good politician's goal is certainly to benefit the community, but the political and governmental system would not be threatened if the crooked deal were not made. Perhaps the community would not be improved as much if another candidate were elected, but such judgments are extremely controversial and difficult to defend. Thus, when a politician acts in ways that would generally be described as wrong, the actions are usually not necessitated by his or her role in the political system. Popular judgment is quite likely to confirm that the politician, despite any countervening obligations, acted wrongly. The role might explain the action but would not make it right.[17]

As a result, the politician is punished while the lawyer is not. But we do not expect the lawyer to get off scot-free. We want the attorney to feel some remorse at having to help free a guilty person. The lawyer who gloats at such an accomplishment will be considered to have a character flaw. Just as with Walzer's politician, doing what is usually morally wrong in order to do good "leaves pain behind, and should do so."[18]

5. Conclusion

Three relationships between universal and special moral obligations have now been uncovered.

1. Special moral obligations can reinforce universal moral obligations (without any clashes between them).

2. Special moral obligations can alter the ordering of moral considerations in ways that yield shifts in what counts as a right action (that is, added weight can be given some moral values so that these values will outweigh others in more cases than would be sanctioned by universal moral obligations alone).

3. Special moral obligations can sanction actions that otherwise (that is, based simply on universal moral obligations) would be clearly immoral.

The dividing lines between these three relationships are not sharp. Indeed, the same obligation can, at different times, fall under more than one category. Medical confidentiality, for example, often simply reinforces the demands associated with ordinary confidentiality. In most situations, the extra care physicians must take not to let personal information about patients slip out poses no conflict with any other special or universal obligations. But medical confidentiality can conflict with universal obligations, as in the case of the psychiatrist whose patient divulges a desire to kill someone. Here, many psychiatrists would argue that their special obligation of confidentiality changes the ranking of obligations and requires that they still not divulge the information, even though ordinary persons who had such knowledge should report it. In short, the relationships between special and universal obligations will be varied and variable.

While the presence of special moral obligations can change the framework for moral decision-making, individual cases must still be examined, and difficult choices must be made. The distinction between universal and special moral obligations and the analysis of the relationships between them provides a structure for decision-making but does not make the decisions for us.

Notes

1. Virtues will be discussed in Chapter IV, rights in Chapter VI.

2. See, for example, Phillip I. Blumberg, "Corporate Responsibility and the Employee's Duty of Loyalty and Obedience: A Preliminary Inquiry," *Oklahoma Law Review*, Vol. 24, no. 3 (August 1971); reprinted in *Ethical Theory and Business*, eds. Tom L. Beauchamp and Norman E. Bowie (Englewood Cliffs, NJ: Prentice-Hall, Inc., 1979), pp. 304–317.

3. The canons and specific rules can be found in the *Code of Professional Responsibility and Code of Judicial Conduct* of the American Bar Association.

4. F.H. Bradley, *Ethical Studies* (Selected Essays) (Indianapolis, IN: Bobbs-Merrill Publishing Co., Library of Liberal Arts, 1951), p. 128.

5. Bradley, p. 101.

6. Bradley, p. 110.

7. Bradley, p. 110.

8. Bradley, p. 139.

9. This is not to say that special moral obligations cannot clash. They can and do. In some cases of euthanasia, the physician's obligation to relieve pain is considered to clash with the obligation not to harm patients. In addition, special obligations based on different roles may clash. A company physician's obligation to the patient may conflict with obligations as an employee.

10. Benjamin Freedman, "A Meta-Ethics for Professional Morality," *Ethics*, Vol. 89 (1978), p. 3.

11. Notice the similarity between alterations in the ordering of values (or considerations) owing to additional role obligations and alterations in the ordering of values owing to changes in circumstances (as in the infanticide case in Chapter II).

12. Freedman, p. 13.

13. Freedman, p. 12.

14. As Walzer notes, Machiavelli deals in depth with the necessity to learn how to do wrong if one is to govern. See Niccolo Machiavelli, *The Prince* and *The Discourses* (New York: Modern Library, 1950).

15. Michael Walzer, "Political Action: The Problem of Dirty Hands," *Philosophy and Public Affairs*, Vol. 2, no. 2 (Winter 1973), p. 165.

16. Walzer, p. 175.

17. A further reason for the difference in judgment might be that the lawyer is not solely responsible for the unfortunate situation. The politician actually lies or makes the crooked deal; the lawyer, though certainly providing aid, does not set the criminal free. It is the judge or jury that must make the final decision.

18. Walzer, p. 172.

Chapter IV

Moral Obligations and Other Action Guides

M oral obligations are, quite obviously, not the only guides to enter people's deliberations. Consider the following partial listing of other factors:

1. Self-interest: In addition to a moral concern for the freedom and welfare of human beings in general, people also take extra care to achieve their particular goals and interests. To act based on self-interest certainly need not represent a violation of moral obligations. Indeed, the capitalist economic system is based on the premise that individuals seeking personal gain can, without consciously attempting to, provide benefits for people in general. (I will have more to say about this in section 4.)

2. Etiquette: Standards of formal behavior such as "Forks go to the left of the plate!" are often guides for deliberation and action. Many of these guides have little to do with morality; it makes no difference to human welfare and freedom where people put the fork in a table setting. Certain precepts of etiquette can, however, have moral underpinnings. Expressions of gratitude, for example, through "Thank You" notes, represent ways to treat people well.

3. Law: Since human beings live in political communities, legal statutes often affect deliberations. Though some laws deal with nonmoral issues (e.g., statutes establishing a particular date for payment of taxes or proclaiming a holiday), many laws, such as those against murder or theft, simply reinforce moral obligations. The law can provide important support for morality by providing systematic enforcement of fundamental obligations.

4. Religion: Many faiths make demands on individuals that are, in essence, moral; the commandments "Thou shalt not kill!" and "Thou shalt not steal!" fit into this category. But religious obligations extend to other areas, such as modes of worship ("Keep holy the sabbath!") and matters of belief ("I am the Lord, thy God, thou shalt not have strange gods before me!")

For many people, there is an important connection between religion and morality. But even when religions do make moral demands on individuals, it is essential to remember that the foundations for religious rules will be quite different. To speak of an obligation not to kill as a religious commandment implies that its foundation is to be discovered within the religious tradition. It will be either a command from God or a principle derived from basic premises of the religion.

Many people would contend that for them, the rules need no more foundation than that God commanded them. This does not mean that there is no foundation for moral rules other than religious authority. In a pluralistic society like ours, it is especially important to understand that moral obligations need not be based solely on specific religious beliefs. Since these guides must apply to all members of the community and since there is no universal religious perspective within our society, a more general grounding is needed.

Of course, our early discussions of basic moral considerations provide the needed foundation. Atheists cannot avoid moral obligations simply because they lack a belief in God. Considerations of welfare and freedom generate reasons for action whether or not one is committed to a religious tradition. Though moral obligations can be given a nonreligious foundation, it is important not to minimize the *support* religion can generate for morality. For many people, moral guides gain their force largely through their connection to religious doctrine.

1. Relationships between Morality and Other Action Guides

As the examples above indicate, there is often significant overlap between moral obligations and other guides. Religion and law make moral demands; etiquette extends beyond table settings to common courtesies and kindnesses; self-interest is often tied to the interests of others.

Even when other guides are not explicitly moral, they are generally consistent with morality. Requirements to worship in certain ways and to hold specific beliefs about the deity may in no way affect how one treats other people. Most importantly, many personal goals, from having fun to making money, can be fulfilled within the dictates of morality.

But conflicts can arise, as the following examples indicate:

1. Law versus universal moral obligations: Take the case of individuals who live in a community with laws that keep one group in an inferior position. Here, the law clashes with the moral demands of equal treatment of human beings. Thus may arise the question of civil disobedience, whether to obey the laws or moral principle.[1]

2. Religion versus special moral obligations: Consider the problem of a devout Catholic physician with a patient who, because of financial as well as psychological difficulties, seeks an abortion. The physician's role obligations to the patient conflict with religious commitment.[2]

3. Self-interest versus universal moral obligations: Consider a business person who is given a choice of providing bribe money or losing a lucrative contract. Obligations of honesty and fairness toward competitors conflict with personal financial interests.

4. Self-interest versus special moral obligations: Take the case of a lawyer who must decide whether to risk his or her practise by defending an unpopular but not necessarily guilty client. Role obligations to the client clash with a concern for personal success.

It is often argued that morality must be supreme, that when it clashes with other factors, the moral obligations must be decisive. Given the variety of other types of action guides, this is a large issue. But a number of general and important points can be raised concerning the supremacy of morality.

First it is necessary to see that issues about the importance of moral obligations (when compared to other action guides) arise at a number of levels. Two general questions can be discerned.

1. Why feel obligated to follow moral action guides? Why be the sort of person who considers moral obligations to be efficacious?

Why consider the guides generated by moral considerations to be weighty? Clearly, this issue emerges at the second stage of moral analysis. It is possible to admit that the well-being and freedom of all people are objective considerations but still contend that guides based on these factors are not terribly weighty when compared to other demands. The discussions in this chapter will focus on this issue of the relative importance of general obligations. The ancient Greeks spoke of a person who took morality seriously as a virtuous individual, that is, one who had developed states of character or character traits that incorporated moral demands. If one does develop appropriate character traits, then moral obligations will automatically be seriously considered in deliberations. In the next section, we will examine Plato's argument for being virtuous.

There is, however, a further question.

2. Even if one does accept moral obligations as pressing, why make them absolutely supreme; that is, why *always* act on them?

If an individual does accept moral obligations as important guides to action, that person will, in general, act on them. But this need not imply that the individual must *always* act morally. In specific situations, a person might deem a little immorality to be acceptable. That is, at stage three, the level of applications of moral obligations, people may find cases in which nonmoral guides seem more pressing.

The issues at the second and third stages of moral analysis are obviously connected; both concern the presumed dominance of morality over other action guides. But there is an important difference. The issue at the general obligation level concerns what is often called the "Why be moral?" question. Why be the sort of person who takes moral obligations seriously? This issue arises prior to — and is more basic than — the question of whether, in every particular case, the dictates of morality must be supreme over other action guides.

Obviously, it is difficult to argue conclusively that there are absolutely no cases in which nonmoral guides outweigh moral obligations. Innumerable challenges can be raised, and each would have to be dealt with. It will be sufficient here to focus on the earlier question, why moral guides ought to be weighty in deliberations. In the process, however, some specific challenges will be examined.

2. Plato and an Argument for Being Moral

The most obvious reason for taking moral obligations seriously is that the considerations on which they are based are real. As Bonnie Steinbock noted, sticking pins in someone causes pain; that fact alone is (or ought to be) sufficient reason for not performing such actions.[3] Obligations to avoid harms to others and to respect people's freedom arise quite simply from an understanding of the nature of moral considerations.

There are some people, however, who are not easily moved by considerations of welfare and freedom when these apply to others. Such people may, unlike the hit-man discussed in Chapter II, accept the existence and relevance of considerations of human welfare and freedom, but they will rank the guides based on these factors as relatively unimportant when compared to guides based on self-interest. Here, the issue is not whether morality exists but whether its demands generally outweigh those of other guides. Can anything be said to these people?

It will not help simply to contend that acting morally is in each person's self-interest. Following moral rules certainly does minimize interpersonal conflicts and skirmishes with social authorities. And to the extent that this is true, such people would agree. But there are obvious cases in which acting immorally can lead to significant personal gain. It is quite easy, for example, to find situations in which stealing poses little risk. Many burglaries are not even investigated, and following the rule against stealing often will not be in an individual's best interests. As a result, morality cannot just be based on self-interest. The response to sceptics concerning the importance of moral action guides must be more complex. As we will see, Plato develops a response that inextricably links personal interests and the interests of others.

In Plato's *Republic*, the challenge to morality is presented by Thrasymachus, who argues that the just person always has the worst of it. (As we shall see, justice is a central virtue to the ancient Greeks. Even though Plato's discussion is framed in terms of justice, the challenge and arguments relate to morality in general.) Thrasymachus contends that "when a partnership is wound up, you will never find that the more honest of two partners comes off with a larger share; and in their relations to the state, when there are taxes to be paid, the honest man will pay more than the other on the same amount of property."[4] This position is elaborated by Glaucon, who notes that justice is accepted because of lack of power to do wrong. Given the institutions of society that provide for punishment for unjust actions, it is generally too risky to act in such a manner. But everyone would forego the principles of justice if he or she could. Indeed, the despot who rules with absolute power, solely for personal gain, without regard to justice or morality is posited as the happiest human. In short, Glaucon concludes that it is best to be bad whenever one can.

This challenge is based on an account of self-interest that reduces it to selfishness, a consideration only for one's own good no matter how this affects others. The challenge is particularly pressing because it does not totally eliminate justice but rather reduces the motivation for it to human weakness. "[Justice] stands half-way between the best thing of all — to do wrong with impunity — and the worst, which is to suffer wrong without the power to retaliate."[5] Many persons are and must be just, but the reason is not because justice itself is valuable but because there is no safe way to act unjustly. In other words, people may perform acts that are just, but they generally do so not out of a desire to be just. The issue, then, is not how people act in specific cases, but what they consider important, what general concerns they take seriously. This raises the question of the weight of moral action guides. How important ought they to be? For Plato, this is a debate over the importance of moral virtues. Why develop character traits (virtues) that lead one to treat moral concerns seriously? For Thrasymachus, there is no value in being the type of person who seeks to be just. There is no reason to develop the virtue of justice.

In response, Plato develops an account of the virtue of justice to indicate its intrinsic importance. The strategy is to discover justice "writ large" in the state and then to apply the account to individuals. Plato's analysis begins with a description of the functions in the state: (1) workers or tradesmen, (2) auxiliaries, and (3) guardians. The workers are the craftsmen, farmers, and others involved in basic production. All combine to maintain the economic life of the community. The auxiliaries are the military services, designed to protect the state. The guardians are rulers in the sense of public decision-makers. These persons define public policy and direct other members in accordance with it.

Plato claims that each person in this ideal state is best suited, (that is, has the natural endowment) for just one social role. Educational programs are devised to determine which persons should be in which roles. If the selection process functions properly, the brightest people will rule, the strongest and most courageous will defend, and those with manual and other economic skills will be producers.

Justice in the state, then, is a matter of each person performing his or her role: "each one should do his own proper work without interfering with others."[6] Injustice would emerge when someone suited for a worker sought to be a guardian. Such an individual's inability to lead would upset the proper balance in the community, and serious problems for the state could result. But Plato is not simply interested in the disasters that might occur from the inappropriate switching of roles. He claims that the best possible situation for the community as a whole emerges when justice is present, when people accept and perform their proper functions. Justice is valuable simply because it enables the community to be as good as it can be — and this will provide important benefits to each member.

Plato's conception of people being naturally suited for only one role, and his extreme emphasis on educational selection for rulers, may not fit a more democratic community. But it is important to remember that Plato's analysis is developed with the ultimate goal of describing justice in the individual. The account summarized above can yield important insights when "writ small."

Plato explains three parts of the human soul (or psyche) corresponding to the three parts of the state.

Part of the Soul	Role	Corresponding Part of State
Nutritive or Appetitive Part	deals with physical needs and desires that maintain individuals (and the species) as living organisms	workers (producers)
Spirited Part	concerns the emotional and psychological aspects of the human personality	auxiliaries (defenders)
Rational Part	involves the intellectual and decision-making capacities of human beings	guardians (rulers)

As in the state, each part of the soul has its own function. The appetitive part must keep the body strong and healthy but must not be so potent that physical desires become all-encompassing. The spirited part, responsible for virtues like courage, must not be so un-bridled that bravery becomes rashness in the face of danger.[7] The only part of the soul that is capable of taking control and making the necessary decisions is the rational part, which must "rule with wisdom and forethought on behalf of the entire soul."[8] When applied to individuals, Plato's view takes on a much more egalitarian tone. Each person has a rational part of the soul; thus, each person can direct his or her life appropriately.

Justice in the individual is directly analogous to justice in the state. Each part of the soul must perform only its proper function. And reason's function as the ruling element leads to Plato's answer to the "Why be moral?" question. The claim that reason must rule with wisdom is an important one, for Plato forges an inextricable link between wisdom and morality. The ultimate knowledge (without which nothing else can be truly known) is knowledge of the good, the moral ideal.[9] To be truly wise is also to be good.

This connection is evident through an examination of what is excluded from the rational part of the soul. Physical desires (for food, drink, sex) are left out because they are features of the appetitive part; emotional and psychological factors (desires for love, personal wealth, and power) are eliminated because they fit under the spirited part. No strictly personal goals, interests, or desires are to be found in the rational part of the soul.

The point is emphasized in Plato's discussion of the life style of the guardians in the state. They are to live in common, with no personal possessions and no permanent personal relationships. Guardians will not take spouses, and any children will be raised in common so that the parents will not develop strong feelings for off-spring. The guardians, whose position explains the rational part of the soul, are to have no strictly personal interests. The result is that guardians are only concerned with the welfare of the community as a whole. They are left to understand the good in the abstract (not in terms of a particular individual's good) and to apply it in the direction of the state. Reason, then, must understand and apply the moral ideal to the actions of the individual.

Plato connects reason with morality in terms of the idea of health. If the rulers of a community are like Plato's guardians, the state will be healthy. Analogously, if an individual is governed by the rational part of the soul, he or she will be healthy. Again, Plato's emphasis on virtues, or character traits, is important. It is a basic characteristic of a rational person to weigh all factors and considerations relevant to an issue. Since these factors will include the impact of one's actions on others, moral obligations will be included. Since reason also weighs factors fairly, without bias, one's personal interests will not be given undue weight. The interests of all will be considered on their merits. Thus, the operation of reason solidifies its connection with morality. But the same operations are also necessary for appropriate decision-making.

Morality is reasonable because people would be better off making decisions according to the above strategy. Just as a state cannot achieve its good without the brightest members ruling, the individual's good is impossible without the rational element in control. To be ruled by the appetites or the spirited part is to create an imbalance and to court disaster. Purely personal desires and interests often blind one to other relevant factors. To act without taking account of all relevant considerations may prove profitable in some situations (as with the despot or the tax-evader), but such actions have a tendency to lead to severe consequences in the long range. Despots often live short lives, and serious tax evasion not only threatens legal reprisals but also weakens the social structure on which all rely. As the analogy to the state indicated, everyone will benefit if individuals act reasonably and, thus, morally. It would be unwise to develop character traits that could ultimately be destructive for both the individual and the community.

Here arises Plato's connection between justice and health.

> Justice is produced in the soul, like health in the body, by establishing the elements concerned in their natural relations of control and coordination, whereas injustice is like disease and means that this natural order is inverted.[10]

Plato's position highlights a vital point. In a broad sense, a healthy individual is one who can function well in his or her environment.

Since morality is based on the needs and limitations of human nature, it becomes a significant feature of the environment and contributes to the survival and benefit of the species. Individuals who do consider the impact of their actions on others will be better able to cooperate and to develop social relationships that yield common benefits. In so far as individuals are mutually dependent, the consideration for each other demanded by moral obligations represents an essential prerequisite for both personal and communal well-being. It makes good sense to say that the person who develops a moral character is "healthy."

The ultimate response to Thrasymachus is that people who have developed character traits that reinforce moral demands will better achieve personal well-being in its various facets because they will reinforce a beneficial social structure. Far from representing a necessary evil, the virtue of justice and morality in general are essential components of human well-being. By developing a commitment to morality, by accepting the intrinsic importance of moral obligations, we are healthier; we can live better. Immorality leaves people at odds with themselves and their environment.

3. Reinforcing the Importance of Moral Guides

Plato's connection between reason, morality, and a healthy individual provides a strong defense of the importance of moral action guides and the attitudes that reinforce them. The argument cannot be ended, however, until moral guides are compared to other types in some detail. The claim that a healthy individual will consider moral action guides to be weighty will be hollow if there are numerous cases in which these guides can be ignored.

In this section, we will consider two cases in which the importance of moral action guides seems questionable. Though the following discussions raise issues at stage three (the application of guides to particular situations), the point is to reinforce Plato's conclusion and to explain how pervasive moral action guides can be. Many cases in which these guides appear to be outweighed by other guides actually represent very different situations.

Consider the following two (possible) exceptions to the supremacy of morality.[11]

Case 1

Predicament: After a dinner party, the host asks a guest how he or she liked the meal. In fact, the guest thought the meal was terrible.

Action: The guest will say (lie) that the meal was fine.

Motivating guide: etiquette.

Case 2

Predicament: An individual has undertaken an obligation (through promising or some other means) to meet a friend at a café for tea. A very important job opportunity arises, however, and an interview is necessary at the time of the café date.

Action: the individual will go to the interview and, thus, not fulfill the obligation.

Motivating guide: self-interest.

These are cases in which the relative weights of the guides involved clearly tend toward the factor portrayed as nonmoral. Few people would argue that they would not or should not perform the action cited. This, of course, provides the force of these examples, for correct actions are supposedly shown to follow from considerations that contradict the demands of morality. If the examples are correct as stated, the importance of moral guides would be brought into question. But because the *actions* described above may be appropriate does not imply that the *motivating guide* cited is correct.

When acting on etiquette is considered appropriate, as in Case 1, the action can also be shown to be in conformity with the dictates of morality. What is the guest worried about in this case? Certainly, compliance with the obvious demands of etiquette may be an issue, but it seems that such demands are not doing all of the work in overriding the obligation not to lie. The feelings of the host are also an issue; moral concerns would urge that one not create unnecessary pain or distress; the generally accepted action in Case 1 calls for kindness instead of truth. The moral wrongness of an inconsequential lie is outweighed by the moral rightness of being kind.

The importance of the moral obligations here can be illustrated in a slightly different case. Suppose the circumstances are exactly the same as in Case 1, but the guest knew that the same dinner would be served again to the mayor. Here, there are strong reasons to find some way to inform the host of any deficiencies or possible improvements in the meal. The motivations to be kind and to follow the dictates of etiquette remain, but other obligations point in the direction of making the truth known.

In each case, the correct action can be given strong moral backing. In the original account of Case 1, morality sanctions the demands of etiquette because of the moral considerations that are relevant there. In the revised case, morality vetoes etiquette's standard response because of more forceful moral obligations that point to a different action.

In Case 2, it can again be argued that the motivating guide is a moral one. There is no reason that one's own welfare and freedom are not properly considered in moral deliberations. Morality demands not self-sacrifice but a concern for human beings in general, and it is impossible to take account of the interests and worth of all affected by an action without including oneself.

To determine whether going to the interview and, thus, breaking a previous obligation is morally acceptable, it is necessary to examine the problem without concentrating on who benefits from the action. Again, consider a slightly revised case. Suppose a friend approached and informed you that she needed a sponsor at an interview to take place at the same time you had promised to meet another person for lunch. If the interview represented an important opportunity for your friend, it is unlikely you would — or should — refuse to help, even if it meant breaking the earlier date. It is quite reasonable that the moral concern for the friend's welfare, in terms of a possible job, should outweigh the moral concern for fulfilling a previous obligation to meet for tea.

Essentially the same situation applies in Case 2. Just because the beneficiary of the action happens to be the same person who must break the previous commitment does not mean that the act suddenly becomes immoral. Rather, self-interest is made consistent with the demands of morality; morality sanctions an action that leads to significant personal benefit.[12] But morality remains the primary reason the action is appropriate. People cannot break promises anytime they would benefit by doing so. Trivial self-interested reasons, like "I just don't feel like going," would not be sufficient. But a self-interested reason becomes significant when personal welfare or freedom would be seriously affected, and it is just these cases in which moral obligations would also justify breaking the commitment.

In Case 1, morality sanctions what is demanded by etiquette because moral obligations also support the action. In Case 2, what appears to be a purely self-interested motivation also has moral backing. The two examples indicate how pervasive moral duties are and how moral guides remain weighty even when, on first sight, other factors seem to motivate a particular action.

There are cases, however, without clear moral factors underlying the decision. We stop at red lights even when the area is completely deserted, because that is the law; and we buy camera equipment because of the personal enjoyment that results. Here, it can be argued that there are no moral issues involved. But morality still lurks behind the scenes. Certainly, situations exist in which there is nothing of moral relevance; but then it is still reasonable to say that morality sanctions actions based on other factors precisely because there is nothing of moral relevance involved. The importance of morality implies only that *in clashes with other factors* moral obligations be decisive. If there is no clash, other guides can have free reign. Once again, let us alter the cases a bit. (1) Would it still be appropriate to stop at a red light in a deserted area when one is transporting an injured person to a hospital? (2) Would it be acceptable to buy camera equipment rather than food for one's hungry child? In these revised cases, morality's role in deliberations is clearly evident; and when moral obligations are pressing, once again they take precedence.

As the examples in this section have shown, morality functions as the ultimate vetoer when there are clashes between moral and nonmoral guides. If moral considerations are not present, other factors may be followed. If moral obligations are relevant, morality may either veto actions in accordance with another type of guide (as when driving through a red light becomes acceptable when a person's life is in danger) or sanction actions consistent with a different guide (as when breaking a relatively minor commitment is acceptable to significantly promote one's welfare).

4. General Moral Obligations and Business

The previous examples indicate how moral obligations serve as a vetoer over other action guides. This further reinforces the importance of taking moral obligations seriously. There is, however, another significant challenge to the importance of general moral obligations. It is often claimed that morality does not enter deliberations in business. Here, self-interest reigns supreme. People who deny morality's efficacy in business affairs do not reject any interest in morality. In other realms (for example, family matters), moral obligations are relevant; but in business, self-interest is king.

Many writers have made such claims. Milton Friedman notes that the only responsibility of business is "to use its resources and engage in activities designed to increase its profits as long as it stays in the rules of the game."[13] Perhaps Theodore Levitt has made the point most strongly. In describing business activities, he notes, "like a good war, it should be fought gallantly, daringly, and above all, *not* morally."[14]

Jack Hirshleifer has developed what may be the strictest defense of self-interest in business. He claims that people are naturally selfish and that economic systems must recognize this. The emphasis on selfishness recalls Thrasymachus's challenge to morality (from Plato's *Republic*). So far, however, there is a significant difference. Thrasymachus was making a normative claim. He was explaining what he felt were correct actions, whether or not anyone actually performed them. Hirshleifer, so far, is making only a factual claim about the way people do, in fact, act.

If talk of humans as selfish is meant to imply (as many of Hirshleifer's comments indicate) that people do not have a concern for morality, the claim can easily be disputed. Most people do take the dictates of morality seriously. The lives and goods of others are respected; promises are kept; the truth is told. These concerns often outweigh pure self-interest; persons avoid killing even when it could be done safely and would yield great personal benefits.

Hirshleifer seems, ultimately, to admit that morality can have an impact. When he describes what he takes selfishness to mean, there seems ample room for moral considerations: "People other than saints simply are more interested in their own health, comfort, and safety than in other people's and will continue to be until the establishment of the Kingdom of God on earth."[15] This motivation may best be called self-interest as opposed to selfishness, since there is no implication that the concern for one's own good functions at the *expense* of others. As previous discussions have shown, there are at least two ways self-interest in the sense described by Hirshleifer can be made consistent with morality. (1) Acting on self-interest may raise no morally relevant issues, as in spending discretionary income on camera equipment, and (2) concern for personal interests may be consistent with moral concerns, as in breaking a date to attend an important job interview. To be especially concerned about one's own good does not imply a lack of concern for the good of others. Nothing in Hirshleifer's description of human motivation requires a general divergence between the demands of morality and actions based on self-interest.

Hirshleifer wants to claim, however, that in business affairs, people act appropriately in ignoring morality and acting solely on self-interest. It is with this normative claim about what counts as proper motivation in business that the challenge to morality's supremacy is made clear. Here, Hirshleifer's point does resemble that of Thrasymachus, though Hirshleifer limits the normative claim solely to business affairs.

It is essential, however, to note the reason for upholding self-interest: In a capitalist system, acting on self-interest works to the advantage of the whole community. "In this system, everyone can be selfish . . . but the market forces them to serve one another's interests, the laborer by working, the employer by paying labor and organizing production, and the consumer by paying for the final product."[16] Levitt echoes the view in claiming that no one will criticize capitalism if "it is a good provider . . . "[17]

Levitt provides another defense for self-interest in a capitalist system: to maintain political and economic freedom.[18] This is the major reason Friedman argues that self-interest is the appropriate motivation in business. The only way to preserve the freedom of individuals is to ensure that the major groups in society — e.g., business and government — remain separate. "The kind of economic organization that provides economic freedom directly, namely, competitive capitalism, also promotes political freedom because it separates economic power from political power and in this way enables one to offset the other."[19] This separation is accomplished by a strict demarcation of roles. It must be government's role — limited though it may be — to deal with pressing social concerns; it is up to business to seek material gain — each person working simply for personal benefit.

It is not essential here to consider the strength of these arguments; whether capitalism can best accomplish the goals cited is not at issue. What is crucial is that the points presented by Hirshleifer, Levitt, and Friedman are *moral* arguments. The contention that morality is irrelevant as an action guide in business is based on principles arising from the moral considerations of human freedom and welfare. The ultimate claim is that an economic system in which people concern themselves only with their own interests will promote best general welfare and freedom.

Morality, then, is necessary to sanction the operation of self-interest in business. This situation recalls that of the lawyer who must defend a guilty client.[20] Considered in isolation, providing aid to people who have committed crimes is likely to be immoral; it is inappropriate to help someone to avoid a reasonable sentence. But when viewed as an essential part of the system in which justice is provided, the lawyer's actions become morally acceptable. The arguments for self-interest in a capitalist system proceed in a similar fashion. Taken in isolation, a concern only for personal interests would often be inappropriate. But in the business sphere, the system has evolved so that human welfare and freedom can be promoted best by just such actions. The result is that what would be immoral in some other situations may be morally acceptable as one part of a process designed to yield important benefits. Far from denying morality's superiority, talk of self-interest as the primary motivation in business is acceptable only because moral sanction can be provided for it.

5. Requirement versus Permissibility

In significant ways, acting on self-interest in business is like an attorney defending a client — even a guilty client — in the system of law. In each case, the moral importance and acceptability of the system in which individuals operate helps to determine what counts as morally appropriate behavior within the system. Once again, the actions are acceptable because morality sanctions them.

Before leaving this issue, it is important to understand that there is a significant difference concerning the type of moral sanction afforded the attorney and the businessperson. As a result of the role, a defense attorney has a special moral obligation to defend clients; the lawyer *must* provide such aid. In business, morality simply permits or allows people to concentrate on their own interests; there is no necessity to operate from such a perspective. As Hirshleifer notes, some individuals may choose to serve others.[21]

The source of the difference in sanctions can be explained in terms of the goals of the systems as a whole. Lawyers function in a system of justice. Our system is arranged on the model of an adversary relationship. The rules are established so that someone who knows the law (that is, the defense attorney) serves as the representative of the defendant's interests in a battle with a prosecutor trying to present the best possible case against the defendant. It is left to the judge or jury — not the attorneys — to determine legal guilt or innocence. In order for the adversary system to work and to stand the best chance of achieving justice, the defense attorney must do the best he or she can to represent the client's interests. There is, then, a requirement that the various lawyers fulfill their roles, and the requirement leads to a pressing special role obligation.

Businesspeople function in an economic system whose fundamental goal (at the social level) is to provide goods. As previous discussions have indicated, the capitalist system is justified in terms of best promoting the general welfare while interfering with individual freedom as little as possible. The system is such that self-interested actions on the part of individuals yield general or community-wide benefits.

Notice that the point of the defense of capitalism is that we can (1) allow individals to seek their own goals and (2) still achieve benefits to the community. Unlike the legal system, the economic system leaves individuals to decide what goals to seek. Morality's sanction of the business system *permits* but does not *obligate* people to seek primarily their own welfare. Indeed, given that a major justification of capitalism concerns its protection for individual freedom, it is essential that people be allowed to determine their own goals.

On the other hand, the complementary argument for capitalism yields significant limits on how far individuals are permitted to seek only their own goods. If a major reason for permitting people to act on self-interest is that the community as a whole can still benefit, then the moral sanction will disappear for cases in which self-interested actions seriously threaten the community or other individuals in it.

Perhaps the most blatant example is provided by Donald Koehn.

> Consider the case of selling an auto to a recently widowed mother of five who is taking herself and her children to her parents' home in San Francisco. Her battered auto breaks down in Kalamazoo, has to be junked, and she needs another.[22]

If self-interest ruled without the need for sanction from morality, it would be acceptable for a used car salesperson to sell the widow a car with a cracked brake line that the salesperson knew — but could not be legally proven to know — would endanger the lives of the passengers. Just about everyone, including businesspeople, would say that such sales tactics go too far. This, of course, implies that self-interest is permissible in business and is sanctioned by morality only as long as other moral obligations are not more pressing.

Industrial pollution represents a situation in which there is harm to the community as a whole. As factories become more congested and production becomes more sophisticated, by-products of production increase both in quantity and impact. To continue to allow companies to dump large amounts of pollutants into the air and water could, and in many cases does, result in severe health hazards. What would be in the self-interest of company stockholders and managers — i.e., dumping pollutants — would also yield significant harms, not benefits, to the community. As a result, it has been necessary to limit self-interested action in these areas. The moral, and legal, sanction for such actions has disappeared.

The moral sanction of self-interest holds only if actions motivated by self-interest will indeed help to achieve the goals expressed for the capitalistic system. The community and its members must benefit or, at least, not be harmed from the actions. When harms clearly outweigh benefits, self-interest will no longer receive the necessary moral sanction, and actions based on self-interest will become unacceptable.

In short, though morality may generally permit self-interested actions in the economic realm, morality retains the authority to overrule or to veto such actions.[23]

The analysis of the claim that self-interest is supreme in business has yielded two important points. (1) Where self-interest is the appropriate motivation for business, it is sanctioned by morality and, thus, is quite consistent with morality's supremacy; and (2) in specific cases, morality still functions as a vetoer — for moral obligations may still outweigh self-interest. Even in economic realms, morality must sanction or veto other guides. But then, morality's role in the business realm is essentially the same as its role in any other realm.

6. Conclusion

The discussions of these first four chapters have sought to explain the foundations of morality, as well as the types and importance of moral obligations. Though many theoretical issues were discussed, most practical problems concerning social and professional issues remain. By clarifying the factors that must be sorted and compared, however, the previous discussions have paved the way for a fruitful examination of specific moral problems.

Notes

1. Philosophical discussions of civil disobedience go back to Socrates. See Plato's *Crito*. More recent discussions include John Rawls, "The Justification of Civil Disobedience," in *Civil Disobedience*, ed. H.A. Bedau (New York: Pegasus, 1969); and Ronald Dworkin, *Taking Rights Seriously* (Cambridge, Mass.: Harvard University Press, 1978), Chaps. 7 and 8.

2. This case is complicated by the confusion over the morality of abortion. If abortion in such cases is immoral, then the physician's role obligations may not extend to performing such actions. For a further discussion of abortion, see Chapter VII, "A Moral Problem: Abortion."

3. See Chapter II, section 3.

4. Plato, *The Republic*, translation and notes by Francis MacDonald Cornford (New York: Oxford University Press, 1945), p. 25.

5. Plato, p. 44.

6. Plato, p. 128. Plato links his account with a common conception of justice as possessing and concerning oneself "with what properly belongs to [one]" (p. 128).

7. Aristotle, Plato's pupil, developed these points by describing virtue as a mean between vices. Courage, for example, is a mean between cowardice and rashness. Of course, it takes practical reason to determine what the mean ought to be. See Aristotle, *Nichomachean Ethics*.

8. Plato, p. 140.

9. See Plato, pp. 212–21, and the allegory of the cave, pp. 227–35.

10. Plato, p. 143.

11. The discussions in this section have benefitted greatly from comments by B.J. Diggs.

12. This does not mean that the previous obligation counts for nothing. There emerges a new obligation to attempt to inform the party of the need to break the date. Again, this obligation arises no matter who the beneficiary of the action is.

13. Milton Friedman, *Capitalism and Freedom* (Chicago: University of Chicago Press, 1962), p. 133.

14. Theodore Levitt, "The Dangers of Social Responsibility," *Harvard Business Review* (September–October 1958), reprinted in *Ethical Theory and Business*, eds. Tom L. Beauchamp and Norman E. Bowie (Englewood Cliffs, NJ: Prentice-Hall, Inc., 1979), p. 141.

15. Jack Hirshleifer, "Capitalist Ethics — Tough or Soft?" *The Journal of Law and Economics*, Vol. 2, pp. 117–18.

16. Hirshleifer, p. 118.

17. Levitt, p. 141.

18. See, for example, Levitt, p. 139.

19. Friedman, p. 9.

20. This case was discussed in more detail in Chapter III.

21. See Hirschleifer, p. 118.

22. Donald Koehn, "A Laissez-Faire Approach to Business Ethics," unpublished, pp. 9–10. There are many other, less blatant examples, such as

hiring people to work in unsafe mines, selling questionably safe food, and discharging pollutants into a community's water supply.

23. Friedman, Levitt, and Hirshleifer are not likely to agree with this claim. They would argue that the free market would eliminate unsafe products and working conditions. Unfortunately, a great many people can be harmed before market forces eliminate the problem. Some consideration for others on the part of businesspersons is necessary so that the harms do not arise in the first place.

Elaborations on
Stages One and Two

Chapter V

Beings Owed Moral Considerations

A re animals owed moral consideration? Is there any sense to saying such consideration applies to plants? Public controversies can hinge on debates over these questions. Is there anything wrong with killing whales if the national economy relies on them? Is it permissible to raise animals in pens so small that the animals cannot turn around? Underlying these issues is the question of whether morality applies to things other than human beings. Once again, specific moral problems demand an investigation of the foundations of morality. We must understand what beings are owed moral consideration before we can fruitfully deal with specific issues at the applications stage of moral analysis.

The question of what beings get moral consideration is often discussed in terms of worth. To ascribe moral consideration to a being signifies that it has value simply for what it is (inherent worth), not just for its usefulness to the deliberator (instrumental worth). The concept of instrumental worth is easily understood. Anything (chairs, land, vegetables, dogs, other human beings) can be useful to a person. The farmer who grows my food, the cow that produces milk for me, and the chair I sit on all are valuable to me because they provide me with benefits.

If this were the only type of worth or value, then I need accept no obligations to these beings and things other than those necessary to maintain their usefulness. For some things, this conclusion seems quite acceptable. I can throw a chair away if it breaks and can no longer serve its purpose. The same cannot be said of a farmer who becomes disabled. The farmer's life is valuable in itself. I must respect that life whether or not it is useful to me. This additional sense of value characterizes inherent worth.

The inherent worth of human beings is based on the considerations of welfare and freedom. Because human beings have needs and interests and can set goals and direct their lives, they have value whether or not they are useful to others. But, though basic moral considerations arose from an analysis of factors common to human beings, that very analysis may require us to extend moral considerations and inherent worth beyond human beings. The features of human nature that led to considerations of welfare and freedom may not be unique to our species. Thus, we may find that the original account of moral considerations as factors that relate to *human beings* in general was incomplete.

1. *Common Views*[1]

Many Western philosophers have argued that only human beings have inherent worth and should be accorded moral consideration. Animals (and, obviously, plants) are not proper recipients. Such a position can be generated from a strict deontological ethics.[2] If beings have inherent worth by being moral agents, then only humans may qualify. Other animals, though they may move on their own and actively seek to satisfy certain needs, seem incapable of understanding the distinction between right and wrong. As a result, they are not held responsible for their actions and are not moral agents.

This type of argument is plausible if rational agency is the only basis for moral consideration. As earlier discussions demonstrated, however, morality must be concerned not only with the ability of individuals to make reasoned decisions but also with the needs and desires of humans as physical beings. If animals resemble humans in terms of physical desires and needs, there may still be grounds for according them moral consideration.

There has been much debate about the similarities between animals and humans even at the level of physical wants and needs.

René Descartes wrote that animals are nothing more than complicated machines. Animals do not really think or feel but are pushed about by purely mechanical responses to external stimuli. It follows that animals are not the sorts of things that could be capable of freedom or of achieving well-being in any way similar to humans. The sense in which animals could be benefitted by our actions would be no different from the sense in which engines run better with regular tune-ups. The animal, like the engine, would not perceive or understand these benefits, but human welfare might well be improved if the animal or the engine ran well. Thus, for Descartes, animals would have only instrumental worth (that is, worth for human beings); they could have no inherent worth.

Much of the reason for Descartes's sharp distinction between human beings and other animals can be traced to his belief that the capacity for any thoughts, feelings, or perceptions requires an immaterial soul.[3] Since only humans possess souls, only humans can think, feel, or perceive — and have inherent worth. Recent physiological evidence about the connection between physical (brain) processes and many perceptions and feelings, combined with a recognition of the physical similarities between humans and other animals, has led many persons to reject Descartes's position. It is now generally believed that many animals can feel and think, at least in some ways. It seems reasonable, then, to contend that animals are capable of well-being similar in some respects to that for human beings.

It has recently become popular to speak of moral considerations as properly extending to animals. Peter Singer, following Bentham, locates the criterion for moral consideration in the capacity to suffer.[4] Since animals can feel pleasure and pain, they have inherent worth. Since plants lack such capacities, they do not have inherent worth and ought not be accorded moral consideration. Joel Feinberg considers the capacity to suffer as one indication that the being in question has interests, and interests (which are "compounded out of *desires* and *aims*, both of which presuppose something like *belief*, or cognitive awareness"[5]) are crucial for a being to be the subject of moral rights. Since Feinberg seems to interpret rights broadly, his view, like Singer's, implies that animals qualify for moral consideration but plants do not.

Is it legitimate to draw the boundary for moral consideration with animals? Kenneth Goodpaster has criticized the emphasis on feelings and beliefs. He contends that Feinberg has arbitrarily limited the scope of interests. "In the face of their obvious tendencies to maintain and heal themselves, it is very difficult to reject the idea of interests on the part of trees (and plants generally) in remaining alive."[6] Goodpaster argues that life, in any form, must be accorded moral consideration.

It is possible to find some support for a life-centered ethics in the moral sensibilities and judgments of many people. The senseless or unnecessary killing of animals is almost universally deplored; every driver will try to avoid the squirrel crossing the highway, even though that squirrel in the middle of nowhere will never be useful to a human being. Our sensibilities also extend to plant life; we consider there to be something wrong with the person who spends the day chopping down trees — even his or her own trees — just to get some exercise.

To be sure, the squirrel may be run over if avoiding it would lead to an accident, and the trees may be chopped down if necessary for heat. Such cases merely prove the point. There must be some significant reason for killing squirrels and trees. These beings are considered to have inherent worth apart from any usefulness to us. It is this worth that must be overridden by careful and judicious reasoning.

It is clear, however, that the sensibilities described above are not yet universal. Some people still support the traditional view explained by Descartes and Kant; others limit inherent worth to humans and animals. Much work must be done to determine whether a moral system ought to ascribe inherent worth to all living things. To deal with this issue, it will be helpful to consider a view that carries a respect for all life as far as possible.

2. Extending Moral Considerations

Paul Taylor has defended a life-centered ethics that denies any superiority of human life over animal and plant life.[7] Such a view demands not simply that all life deserves some respect but that all life has the *same* inherent worth. Taylor often speaks of the traditional anthropocentric view (of Descartes and Kant) as the position opposed to his egalitarian system. It appears, however, that Taylor's view and the traditional perspective represent opposite extremes, with more moderate positions (like Feinberg's and Singer's) possible in between. Indeed, much evidence indicates that people's actual attitudes do not fall into either extreme. As the examples concerning the squirrel and trees showed, many people do accept obligations concerning nonhuman life. On the other hand, people also seem to consider human life to have more worth than nonhuman life. An analysis of Taylor's view will indicate what conclusions we must draw concerning beings that are owed moral consideration.

Taylor develops a biocentric outlook on nature, "a coherent, unified, and rationally acceptable 'picture' or 'map' of a total world view."[8] He expects such an outlook to provide the philosophical perspective appropriate for a respect for nature. The biocentric outlook is based on (1) the common membership of all living things in the earth's community of life, (2) the fact that each organism is a teleological center of life, (3) the interconnectedness of all types of life, and (4) the denial of human superiority. I will examine the first two points to see in what ways they provide content for claims of the inherent worth of all living things. A discussion of the last two points is saved for the ensuing sections.

Taylor emphasizes the similarities of origin of all life on earth, the common environmental problems faced by all life, and the similar requirements for survival imposed on all biological life. He states, "In this light, we consider ourselves as one with them, not set apart from them."[9] In satisfying its needs, each species shares a common home and is a part of a community of life. Taylor also points out the uniqueness of each life — not simply each human life. Each living thing is a system striving (even if not consciously) for its particular well-being.[10] This is what Taylor means by calling organisms "teleological centers of life."[11]

These points capture the foundations for a respect for life. Life in general is very special. We have yet to discover evidence of life outside our planet, and despite our scientific prowess, we are still unable to create life out of inanimate matter. These facts may change, but that will not alter the special nature of individual living things; each particular living thing exists only once. Despite the possibility of cloning, differences in environmental and developmental conditions will ensure some respects in which each life is unique. Every living thing battles innumerable enemies to maintain its existence. The battle itself seems noble, whether it be the struggle of a person wracked with cancer or the emergence of the first plant amid the destruction of Mt. Saint Helens's blast.

Thus, there are reasons for ascribing inherent worth to animals and plants. But it is important to remember that a life-centered ethics not only must extend the boundary for beings with inherent worth beyond humans but also must draw the line at living things. There is a sense in which each rock is unique, but we would not ascribe inherent worth to rocks. The reason seems to be that nonliving things are not (uniquely) striving to achieve their well-being. Taylor's talk of organisms as teleological centers of life is crucial here and emphasizes the fragility and nobility of life. What is most important about the features common to all living things is also uniquely possessed by living things.

This point can be emphasized through an analysis of one way that value (though not necessarily intrinsic value) has been extended to nonliving things. Mark Sagoff speaks of ascribing value to the natural environment in such a way that waterfalls and mountains (and not just the living things in or on them) are to have value. The reason is that these natural things express qualities and virtues that we respect. But there is a significant difference between expressing qualities and having capacities. A mountain can express qualities of nobility, strength, and freedom only given a certain type of perceiver. To relatively small beings (like humans) who are threatened by severe cold and who find climbing difficult, mountains certainly are strong, noble, and free in an expressive (aesthetic) sense. The basis for ascribing value to living things, however, is not owing to our perceiving them in a certain way but owing to the capacities that living beings have in themselves. (As Goodpaster notes, "As if it were human interests that assigned to trees the task of growth or maintenance!"[12]) Since the mountain's value is ultimately grounded in our relationship to it, it does not have inherent worth. Sagoff seems to accept this, for he speaks of the obligation to nature that he describes as an obligation "to our national values, to our history, and, therefore, to ourselves."[13]

The various points raised above do explain and, in effect, provide justification for a life-centered ethics. Moral reasons can be raised against running over a squirrel or chopping down trees for exercise. These beings are owed (and generally seem to receive some) respect for what they are, because of capacities and features that make them living things. Much of what we value in human beings is also found in other forms of life — and only in other forms of life. What is at issue here are the factors about each being as a type of life; each type, on its own, possesses features sufficient for ascribing inherent worth to it. To deny this is to ignore certain facts about ourselves and other beings.

3. Inherent Worth and Basic Moral Considerations

So far, support for the inherent worth of living things has been gleaned from examples of our moral sensibilities and from two features of Taylor's biocentric outlook: the common needs of all life and the nature of living things as teleological centers. The ultimate foundation for both the sensibilities and the outlook can be analyzed in terms of the basic moral considerations of welfare and freedom.

These considerations arose from certain facts about human beings. Because humans are living and active beings, they have certain biological, emotional, and spiritual needs. Because humans are deliberative beings capable of making choices, freedom from others becomes valued. What is crucial, however, is that animals and plants share a number of needs and capacities of human beings. Animals can also deliberate in certain ways (consider a mouse solving a maze) and can make some choices. Both animals and plants have biological needs (for example, for nourishment) that are similar to those of human beings. Welfare considerations, then, also apply to animals and plants, while considerations of freedom may be owed animals in some respects.

Each living being has a good of its own; it can be benefitted or harmed, nurtured or killed by human action. These facts are illuminated through certain features of Taylor's biocentric outlook. The similarities of origin of all life explains in part the similarities of biological needs. The teleological features of living things emphasizes that all such beings actively seek their good. Again, what counts as the good of each living being will exhibit strong similarities to the good of all other living things. It appears that there is no way to avoid extending welfare considerations to all living things. If the appropriate ascription of such consideration is a ground for claiming that a being has inherent worth, then all living things have such worth.

The inherent worth accorded animals and plants is ultimately grounded in the fact that these living beings are the legitimate subjects of moral considerations (especially welfare considerations). It does not follow, however, that we must ascribe equal inherent worth to all living things. The need for some distinctions in levels of inherent worth can be seen through an analysis of the third aspect of the biocentric outlook: the interconnectedness of all life.

The issues discussed so far differ greatly from Taylor's emphasis on the interconnectedness of organisms in the earth's environment. As Taylor notes, organisms in our system are mutually dependent. "In the long run, the integrity of the entire biosphere of our planet is essential to the realization of the good of its constituent communities of life, both human and nonhuman."[14]

Taylor's emphasis on the natural world as an organic system does not explain or justify claims of the inherent worth of other species. Here, respect for other beings depends on their value to the ecosystem as a whole (on which all species depend). Any value arising from this situation will not be intrinsic value but value as a means. We need plants both for the production of oxygen and for food. If the worth of other species is based on such value, then they may be treated and used essentially as a means. Individual plants will be protected only in so far as they are necessary to maintain the ecological balance essential for human existence. It is just this view that Taylor seems to be battling against.

In addition, viewing the world as an organic system points in two directions. Certainly, species are mutually dependent, but there is also a good deal of competition among living things. The interdependence indicates the need to use other species — even to kill other species — for survival. Though possessing inherent worth, animals that eat our food and weeds that strangle our crops are, nonetheless, threats. The interconnectedness of species in our ecosystem seems not so much to explain the inherent worth of all life but to emphasize the way all species can and often do use others as a means, and compete for scarce resources.

Our ethics cannot ignore either the inherent worth of all life (based on points like uniqueness, similarities of origin and needs, and teleological factors) or the ways species use others and compete for survival. Important questions arise concerning how to balance a competitive, adversary relationship against the inherent worth of our competitors. The question of human superiority is crucial in deciding many of these issues. As Hartshorne notes, "Either our use of other animals and of plants as food is unethical, or our ethics assumes the greater importance of an individual of our own species than at least some of the nonhuman individuals in nature."[15]

4. Distinctions Among Types of Life

A major feature of Taylor's biocentric outlook is the rejection of human superiority. Such a view threatens many of our basic moral judgments. We not only kill (harvest) wheat for food but also kill (chop down) trees for nonsurvival needs, such as paper. Though it is reasonable to argue that we should do as little killing as possible to provide goods such as paper, it does seem permissible to kill trees when necessary to satisfy legitimate demands for such products. Though killing animals for food is quite controversial, there do seem to be cases in which the lives of animals can legitimately be sacrificed for the welfare of human beings. City rats are destroyed to provide a safer living environment for humans. If killing laboratory animals is necessary to provide the essential ingredient for a drug that would cure human paralysis, it seems permissible to kill the animals. All of these actions and judgments are based, at least in part, on the assumption of human superiority.

Perhaps the most forceful case to illustrate the need for justified differences in levels of inherent worth concerns a life-saving choice. Suppose, as you are walking along an empty beach, you see a human being and a dog both struggling in the water. Since you are good swimmer, you can attempt a rescue, but it is likely that you will only be able to save one. In such situations, you are quite likely to save the human being. Indeed, the judgment that saving the human being is correct is an extremely strong one. The basis for this moral judgment, however, must be an intuition about the higher level of worth accorded human beings. In all other respects, the situations are identical. It is, of course, possible that the intuitive judgment that one ought to save the human being first (rather than, for example, flipping a coin) is incorrect. To determine its acceptability, we must examine whether there are grounds for differences in levels of worth.

The question is whether humans have *more* inherent worth than other living things. A belief in human superiority does not imply, as Taylor sometimes notes, that "no intrinsic value is to be placed on the good of other animals . . . their well-being imposes no moral requirement on us."[16] To defend a less extreme position than either Taylor's egalitarian view or the opposing anthropocentric view, one must argue first that it makes sense to speak of grading inherent worth and then that human beings are due more inherent worth than other living things.

While individual beings have (or lack) inherent worth, such worth is ascribed because the being is a member of a species or type. This marks the distinction between worth and merit or desert. Individuals gain merit based on *personal* accomplishments; individuals have inherent worth based on the type of being they are. In Taylor's discussions (echoed in sections 2 and 3 here), living organisms have inherent worth as forms of life. As a result, a fundamental distinction is drawn between living and nonliving things. The question is whether finer distinctions among different types of living things can be made.

All living beings share vegetative capacities, but some beings are also active and conscious. Others are not only active and conscious but also are moral agents. The distinctions here correspond roughly to the biological divisions among plants, animals, and human beings. It is important to note that this correspondence is very rough. There may be questionable cases concerning which species ought to count as conscious and active, and which ought to be considered moral agents. To simplify the discussions here, I will speak throughout of plants as representing vegetative life, animals as conscious and active life, and humans as moral agents.

Plant life, though certainly possessing inherent worth as life, is not conscious, not capable of feeling pleasure and pain, and not capable of self-directed activity in any sense. Animals, simply because of the type of being they are, do possess some (or all) of these capacities. With respect to how we should treat these beings, the differences in capacities do not mean simply that our obligations to animals extend in different ways — it makes little sense, for example, to speak of an obligation to avoid causing emotional pain to plants. In addition, we are likely to believe that in a clash of similar obligations (for example, the obligation to protect life), the life of an animal ought to be protected over the life of a plant. The implication is that the animal's inherent worth outweighs that of the plant because the animal is more than just vegetative life.

Such a conclusion follows nicely from the application of basic moral considerations to various beings. There are, after all, differences in the extent to which the considerations apply. Welfare considerations, in a fundamental biological sense, must be accorded all life. But animals also seem capable of achieving well-being in an emotional sense, and animals, unlike plants, are capable of self-directed activity and, thus, of appreciating realms of freedom. (Of course, humans are capable of well-being in further, intellectual and aesthetic senses, and because of additional intellectual abilities, humans can value new realms of freedom.) In short, while each living being must be accorded some moral consideration and, as a result, has inherent worth, the extent to which moral considerations can be applied will vary from species to species. Some beings will be capable of well-being and freedom in more ways than others and, thus, will have moral considerations ascribed to them in additional respects. Since inherent worth is linked to the ascription of moral considerations, differences in the range of applicable moral considerations can legitimately be translated into different levels of inherent worth.

Such a judgment does not demand that we consider the capacities of animals to be more valuable than those of plants. As Taylor notes, talk of value at this point is relative to the good of various species; each species possesses those capacities valuable for the achievement of its particular well-being. But the nature of the good a being can achieve will be dependent on the capacities of the being. Thus, differences in the range of capacities of various species can lead to differences in worth. The fact that animals are conscious and active beings while plants are not can be translated into differences in (1) levels of goods that each species is capable of and, thus, (2) levels of inherent worth owed these beings.[17]

5. Levels of Worth and Human Superiority[18]

An understanding of the range of the various types of moral considerations leads to the recognition that not all considerations will
apply to every species. Since the appropriateness of according considerations will depend on the capacities of the species (which determine the nature of each species' good), and since moral consideration
is the ground for ascribing inherent worth, it is possible to develop the
following principle for sorting levels of inherent worth. A type of
being that (1) has the capacities (relevant for ascribing moral considerations) of other beings and (2) has additional capacities that
result in the ascription of further types of moral considerations to it
ought to have more inherent worth.[19]

The principle provides a way to distinguish differences in kind
among types of beings. If a species is capable of well-being not simply
in terms of physical survival but also in terms of feeling pleasure and
pain, a variety of moral considerations are appropriately ascribed to
it. Levels of inherent worth will depend on the range of such considerations that apply, and this will be determined by the capacities
of the species.

These differences, then, do not transfer simply into differences in
degree. Living things will not be ascribed higher levels of inherent
worth on the basis of possessing a common capacity in a more refined
or more developed form. The capacity to be pleased by a wider range
of foods (because one's digestive system is capable of handling the
variety) does not alter the fact that humans and animals can both
achieve well-being in this general way. Differences in inherent worth
emerge only when grounds for new and additional considerations are
present.

What makes this principle most reasonable is that it is simply an
extension of the strategy used for determining grounds for ascribing
any inherent worth. Factors such as similarities of origin and teleological features amount to differences in kind between living things
and other things, for these features highlight capacities (1) that only
living beings possess and (2) that lead to moral consideration. The
principle described above applies the same idea. If, based on the

capacities of the beings themselves, relevant differences in kind can be discovered among living things, then differences in levels of inherent worth can be posited.

The principle, of course, does not imply that we always favor beings with more inherent worth. Other factors may also be important. The principle does lead to a *presumption* in favor of beings with more inherent worth. Once again, it is important to distinguish between the second and third stages of moral analysis. The principle establishing different levels of inherent worth represents a general obligation (stage two) that can, in particular situations (stage three), give way to other obligations.

It is interesting to note that in many ways, principles of the type described above provided the basis for those people who posited differences in inherent worth among human beings. Aristotle argued that slaves lacked the capacities for governing their own lives; aristocrats claimed that only the nobility were capable of appreciating the arts and other "higher" activities; White supremacists contended that Blacks lacked capacities for sophisticated thought; male chauvinists argued similarly with respect to women.

What is most revealing is that critics of such views have accepted the principle concerning grounds for differences in inherent worth but have argued that it simply did not apply in the above cases. Barbarians, peasants, Blacks, and women are not lacking in any of the capacities cited and thus do not have less inherent worth.[20] As noted earlier, there seem to be no relevant differences among types of human beings.

There are, of course, differences among particular human beings that can lead to differences in some judgments. One may be a better musician, another a better person (for example, in terms of sharing with others). Such differences do affect considerations of merit (as Taylor emphasizes), but there remains a sense of equal inherent worth based on the type of being one is. Traditional discussions of worth emphasized this: barbarians, women, and Blacks were considered inferior simply on the basis of being members of a certain type. As noted above, critics of these views contended that the categories did not correspond to differences in capacities. Questions of inherent worth concern which beings deserve moral consideration simply for the kind of being they are — not for what they do with the abilities that make them what they are.

Though no significant differences can be found among types of human beings, the same cannot be said for the relationship between animals and plants. Previous discussions indicated that relevant differences in kind, relating to the ascription of moral considerations, do exist between these types of life, and the above principle explains the grounds for distinguishing between the inherent worth of animals and plants.

A distinction between human beings and other animals can be made on the basis of those capacities associated with personhood in terms of moral agency (for example, rationality, complex communicative skills, and understanding of moral values).[21] These capacities combine to make human beings responsible agents, able to understand and to judge right and wrong as well as to develop and to act on long-term goals and plans. No other beings possess such abilities. Human beings and other animals share the capacities for consciousness, for feeling pleasure and pain, and for self-directed activity. To be sure, some animals may move faster or in different ways from humans, but these are differences in degree. The capacity for personhood in the sense of moral agency is an additional capacity of human beings that is relevant for ascribing moral consideration. Such a capacity yields a significant, additional feature of the good that human beings are capable of. The ability to formulate and to follow a plan of life can imply, among other things, that the freedom of moral agents must be respected to a greater extent than that of other animals. It is appropriate and necessary to limit the activities of many animals precisely because they cannot interact with us at the level of responsible agents. As a result, it is reasonable and consistent to ascribe more inherent worth to beings possessing a capacity for responsible action than to other beings.

Again, this is not to say that the capacity for personhood is more valuable than those abilities possessed by other animals, but simply that these are additional capacities possessed by a being that already has the general capacities of other types of life.[22] The presence of the capacity for moral agency makes human beings significantly different — but not morally superior — to other living things. Humans are not better beings than animals in the sense that animals should be judged morally deficient in comparison to humans. The absence of certain capacities does not imply that animals are bad. Rather, since humans do have capacities for moral agency, moral considerations must be ascribed to them in additional ways. The distinction between human beings and other animals is forged in the same way as the distinction between plants and animals: by discovering differences in kind among types of life. Just as the distinction between animals and plants was not taken as evidence that plants are worse beings than animals, differences between human beings and other animals need not indicate the moral superiority of humans.

As a result, much of what Taylor demands with his life-centered ethic can be upheld even if distinctions among types of life are made. Once the inherent worth of all life is recognized, we can accept that "we are morally bound (other things being equal) to protect or promote [the good of wild animals and plants] for *their* sake."[23] What must be given up, once levels of worth are distinguished, is Taylor's egalitarianism among various species. A comparison simply in terms of the capacities relevant to the ascription of moral consideration — the same strategy used to distinguish living from non-living beings — can justify differences in levels of inherent worth among beings.

6. Conclusion

The discussions here have provided a framework for dealing with the relative worth of various types of life. Specific questions, such as exactly when human interests outweigh the obligations people have to respect the lives and welfare of nonhuman beings, remain. It is possible that differences in levels of inherent worth would still not sanction many current practises concerning our treatment of other living things. To what extent is it permissible to raise and to kill animals for food? What conditions ought dairy animals be provided? When is medical or psychological research on animals permissible? How do we weigh economic survival of Alaskan islanders against the lives of seals, whose pelts provide the major source of income for the islanders?

The discussions here do not, and were not intended to, determine how big a difference there is in levels of worth among beings. Once the grounds for our obligations are clear, there is still much work to be done in specific cases where these obligations clash. The goal of this chapter was to indicate how moral obligations to nonhuman beings arise. Since people have not always recognized such obligations, their acceptance yields new problems. A respect for all living things, though common in many cultures, was not a fundamental tenet of ours. On the traditional anthropocentric view espoused by Descartes and Kant, there are few moral dilemmas concerning the use of animals. Thus, for many people, questions about the permissibility of eating meat or using animals in experiments represent new moral dilemmas. Once we understand the relevant similarities between human beings and other living things, our newly discovered obligations yield numerous cases in which we must take account of the interests of other beings.

Notes

1. Many points in the following sections were presented in my article "Inherent Worth, Respect, and Rights," *Environmental Ethics*, Vol. 5, no. 3 (Fall 1983), pp. 257–270.

2. See Chapter I, "Moral Considerations."

3. See, for example, *Meditations on First Philosophy*, *Principles of Philosophy*, Principle CLXXXIX; and *Passions of the Soul*, Part I (especially pp. 331–56); all in *The Philosophical Works of Descartes*, trans. Elizabeth S. Haldane and G.R.T. Ross (New York: Cambridge University Press, 1969).

4. See Peter Singer, *Animal Liberation* (New York: A New York Review Book, Random House, 1975), Chap. 1.

5. Joel Feinberg, "The Rights of Animals and Unborn Generations," in *Rights, Justice, and the Bounds of Liberty* (Princeton: Princeton University Press, 1980), p. 168.

6. Kenneth Goodpaster, "On Being Morally Considerable," *The Journal of Philosophy*, Vol. 75, No. 6 (June 1978), p. 319.

7. Paul W. Taylor, "The Ethics of Respect for Nature," *Environmental Ethics*, Vol. 3 (Fall 1981), pp. 197–218.

8. Taylor, p. 205.

9. Taylor, p. 207.

10. The common features of all living things have been emphasized by a number of writers. As noted above, Goodpaster argues that the only nonarbitrary criterion for moral consideration is being alive. (See Goodpaster, p. 310.) Charles Hartshorne notes the biological connections among types of life; see "The Rights of the Subhuman World," *Environmental Ethics*, Vol. 1 (Spring 1979), pp. 49–60.

11. Taylor, p. 210.

12. Goodpaster, p. 319.

13. Mark Sagoff, "On Preserving the Natural Environment," *The Yale Law Journal*, Vol. 84, No. 2 (1974); reprinted in *Today's Moral Problems* (2nd ed.), ed. Richard Wasserstrom (New York: Macmillan Publishing Co., 1979), p. 620.

14. Taylor, p. 209.

15. Hartshorne, p. 54.

16. Taylor, p. 215.

17. The distinction between animal and plant life is significant (and perhaps easier to defend than the distinction between human beings and other animals). It is interesting to note that, in arguing that all types of life have the same inherent worth, Taylor only mentions the distinction between human beings and other animals, calling this distinction "an irrational bias in our own favor." (Taylor, p. 207.) The fact that we do make a distinction between animals and plants, however, seems to indicate that there is more behind divisions in levels of worth.

18. Taylor has replied to some of the points presented in this section in "Are Human Beings Superior to Animals and Plants?" *Environmental Ethics*, Vol. 6 (Summer 1984), pp. 149–60.

19. Individual members of various species may not possess all the capacities or features associated with their type. Specific judgments may be necessary here, but they seem not to threaten general accounts of the worth to be accorded the species in question. For a discussion of the inappropriateness of questioning general judgments because of exceptional cases, see L.B. Cebik, "Can Animals Have Rights? No and Yes," *The Philosophical Forum*, Vol. XII, No. 3 (Spring 1981), pp. 254–56.

20. In many historical instances, the situation was more complex. Since Blacks, for example, were not provided the same educational opportunities and training as Whites, it was easier to argue that they were less intelligent

(since intelligence is not entirely a natural capacity) than Whites. The fundamental question, however, is whether Blacks had the same potential for intellectual development. Here the bigot's argument fails. There are no relevant differences between the races in terms of potential for development.

21. The capacities for moral agency are, strictly speaking, only possessed by mature human beings. It may be reasonable, however, to ascribe similar worth to children because they are potential moral agents.

22. Taylor fails to see the importance of describing differences in inherent worth solely in terms of capacities relevant for ascribing moral consideration. In discussing moral agency as a possible basis for distinguishing the worth of animals from that of human beings, he considers an emphasis on this capacity to imply the *moral superiority* of human beings. (See Taylor, "The Ethics of Respect for Nature," p. 213.)

23. Taylor, "The Ethics of Respect for Nature," p. 198.

Chapter VI

Human Rights as
Action Guides

A ppeals to human rights have a long history. The concept has been influential in efforts to extend full moral and legal protection to more and more members of the community. From the Magna Charta's extension of power from monarch to nobles, to the demands by colonists for representation, claims to rights have been at the forefront of efforts to mold a democratic society. In the United States, the twentieth century has seen civil rights and women's rights movements extend protection beyond White males. Today, throughout the world, human rights are invoked as the basis for protecting members of minority groups, the powerless, and the suppressed. Organizations such as Amnesty International base efforts for political prisoners on concerns for human rights. The importance of human rights in political events world-wide cannot be denied.

Demands for rights are common, so common that the concept is applied in almost any setting. What are we to say about claims that trees or rocks should have rights? While the concept of animal rights sounds reasonable, the issues associated with extending 'rights' to cows and dogs seem different from earlier demands that the rights accepted for males be extended to women as well. Rights were originally elaborated concerning proper treatment of human beings, and it is there that discussions must start. As argued in Chapter V, there are good reasons to consider all living things to have inherent worth — though there can be different levels of worth. Appeals to rights have been especially influential in attempts to extend the highest level of worth to all human beings. In this Chapter, I will examine human rights as expressing that high level of worth owed human beings.

There is something very special about claims of *human* rights. These demands arise within the context of institutions, roles, and relationships that exist in any human society. Differences among people in terms of physical appearance and abilities, intellectual capacities, emotional stability, and family background and influence will often lead to significant differences in opportunities, roles, and rewards. How far should we allow these differences to affect each individual's opportunities and social power? Should intelligence or family history determine who governs a community? Should the wealth of one's family determine the level of education one can achieve? Human rights theorists have long argued that people should be treated equally with respect to many fundamental social opportunities and powers — even if there are significant differences among people.

1. Historical Survey

Despite their popularity in American political and social history, rights have not always had a favored place in the Western intellectual tradition. In the seventeenth century, John Locke spoke of the natural rights that human beings were granted by God.[1] These included a basic liberty of thought and action as well as control over one's person and property. Locke was defending democratic political institutions, and his views provided a theoretical framework for a shift in the relationship between individuals and their government. Locke's conception of government as a trustee of the people and as subject to the people reversed a great deal of earlier history and theory. The new account of the subservience of government emerged as an implication of Locke's reliance on people's rights, rights that were independent of and had to be respected by government.

Early theories of rights often relied on interpretations of divine will. Locke felt rights were bestowed by a supernatural being, and this was the reason that neither individuals nor governments could ignore them. The religious foundation is evident in the American Declaration of Independence, which proclaims that "all men are endowed by their Creator with certain inalienable rights." Jefferson's debt to Locke emerges in the phrasing of key passages of the Declaration of Independence. But it was and remains difficult to prove statements concerning divine foundations for human rights, given the variety of religious beliefs and the differences in interpretation within religions. As a result, many people began to feel that rights were bogus moral commodities. If theories of rights could be convincing only to people holding a specific religious perspective, then rights would not function as universal demands. Nonbelievers could ignore claims based on rights. The difficulties for theories of rights intensified, and in the nineteenth century, Jeremy Bentham called rights "nonsense on stilts."[2] This view was widely held by philosophers through the early part of the twentieth century. Unfortunately, criticisms of human rights theories lead to threats against one of the most potent arguments for protecting individuals — especially those who lack social or political power — against established authority.

During the second half of this century, rights have once again become an important part of philosophical analyses of morality. No doubt this is partly due to the atrocities committed during World War II. The attempt to annihilate an entire people is something so clearly wrong that it revives the need to explain and to protect certain basic rights that all people share regardless of race, sex, religion, or national origin. The discrimination faced by women, Blacks, and other minorities in the United States has further emphasized the need for a well-developed and effective theory of rights. Rights theories still provide one of the most fervent expressions of the value of the individual against government, against social custom, and against majority opinion. Popularity does not, however, guarantee correctness or continued influence. Though appeals to rights may now be common, it is important to understand their nature and basis if they are to remain forceful.

2. Rights as a Type of Action Guide

Invoking a right is a demand that others respect a particular moral obligation. When an individual claims a right to free speech, the intent is to get others to uphold the obligation not to interfere with public expression.

Each right immediately invokes general guides to action. Some of these are obvious; a right to life quickly generates an obligation not to kill. The right to life may also involve an obligation to give or to get aid in life-threatening emergencies. Sometimes the scope of a right may be controversial; does the right to life imply that the poor are owed resources from those better-off? At any rate, a right may encompass a whole range of general obligations relating to ways the value in question ought to be respected. In short, rights function at the second stage of moral analysis; they express ways moral considerations must be dealt with in deliberations on action.

As noted in earlier discussions, all action guides, even those associated with rights, yield only presumptions of treatment. It is *presumed* that each moral guide will be acted on, but there will be cases in which specific guides will have to be rejected in favor of others. An individual may have and claim a right to life as he or she is attacking you with a dagger. But your obligation to preserve that life can be outweighed by a legitimate concern for your own survival. In other words, a right does not determine action until it is clear from an analysis of the facts of a specific case that the right is the most significant one in that case.

Rights simply express the obligations associated with moral action guides from a different perspective.[3] So far, in discussions of rules, principles, or even virtues, the focus has been on the individual *who must act*. These guides require concern for certain beings. Those individuals can, as a result, *expect* treatment consistent with the guides. Rights express ways people can expect to be treated; they arise from the perspective of the individuals *who will be affected by the actions*. This is why, when a right is invoked, it is usually as a demand that *others* deliberate and act in a certain way. To claim a right to freedom of religion is to demand that others accept the obligation not to interfere with one's choice of religious affiliation. Again, the sense in which rights, and moral action guides in general, are presumptions emerges. Individuals can presume that, as long as people are concerned to act morally, the obligations associated with rights will be upheld.

If sufficiently strong reasons for acting against a right are present

in a particular case, the guide associated with the right will legitimately give way. But even if, for example, it is permissible to interfere
with an individual's freedom in order to prevent serious but uninten-
tional harm to others, the individual restricted still retains a right to
liberty. The right is always with the bearer. The freedom of that person must still be considered seriously in deliberations on action —
and must be acted on if no relevant and sufficiently strong reasons not
to exist. The right, as a general obligation, still exists, even when it is
not acted on. Once again, the difference between the second and third
stages of moral analysis must be recognized. Action guides never
disappear; their relevance and force as guides are not affected even if
they are appropriately rejected when applied to a particular situation.
The right to life is not weakened when someone kills in self-defense.

What counts as a relevant and sufficiently strong reason for not
upholding a right still needs to be determined. Though this issue will
ultimately be resolved after a discussion of the content of human
rights, it is on the question of justifiable reasons for overriding obligations that rights are distinguished as a *special type* of action guide. For
moral guides as a whole, many factors will enter into the reasoning for
overriding rules. For example, as moral consideration is extended to
nonhuman animals and plants, the nature of the being in question will
become relevant. Killing plants to save or feed animals and people will
be acceptable. Rights, however, are often described as the most important moral commodity in existence. Wasserstrom describes rights as
"the strongest kind of claim that there is."[4] In other words, the types
of reasons that will override a presumption of right will be quite
limited.

The obligations associated with rights will very seldom be
justifiably rejected. To have a right is to be worthy of the highest level
of moral consideration that is accorded and, thus, to possess the
strongest possible presumption of treatment respecting the object of
the right. This is the essence of Wasserstrom's point. There are many
moral obligations. These obligations will yield guides of varying
strengths. The moral rule against intentionally killing another human
being will be stronger than the obligation to be kind to one's
neighbors. Those obligations that are associated with rights will represent the strongest type of moral demand that can be made. Thus,

claims to right will be the most powerful that an individual can muster.

This special status makes rights both potent and popular. Thus, in recent years, minorities and women have demanded not just moral consideration or respect, but moral (and legal) rights. Claims to human rights properly highlight certain fundamental obligations owed human beings. It is not surprising then that rights have for centuries been at the heart of efforts to end political, religious, and social oppression. There are, of course, times when persons or groups make illegitimate claims to rights, but it is clear that the injustices that led to civil rights, women's rights, and gay rights have involved violations of some fundamental and crucially important moral obligations. Once members of these groups demonstrated that their demands were matters of right, they had the most forceful moral argument they could make.

3. The Basis of Human Rights

Once we recognize that rights are a special type of moral action guide, it is possible to grapple with questions about the content of human rights. Claims to rights are extremely popular, but exactly what can be claimed as a matter of right? Locke spoke of rights to life, liberty, and property. The United Nations' Universal Declaration of Human Rights expanded the number to include rights to a nationality, to equal pay for equal work, and to periodic holidays with pay. A number of civil liberties organizations now claim that employees have a right to privacy that prohibits mandatory drug testing. How can we determine what counts as a right? This issue is often discussed in terms of the search for a fundamental human right. Any specific rights that can be derived from the fundamental right would qualify as human rights.

Two general strategies for describing the fundamental right have been employed. Some (e.g., Dworkin and Richards) have spoken of a fundamental right to equal treatment.[5] Others (e.g., Melden and Mackie) have argued for the right to pursue one's interests.[6] In a version of this strategy, Wasserstrom and Vlastos have spoken of rights to well-being and freedom.[7]

Clearly, both strategies provide accounts that can encompass many specific rights. The right to pursue one's interests, for example, can be elaborated in terms of rights to determine one's religious affiliation, to free speech, to freedom of assembly, and to free choice of occupations. Wasserstrom's and Vlastos's strategy of describing fundamental rights to well-being and freedom simply incorporate basic considerations of welfare and freedom, the foundations for any moral action guide, as the content of rights. Much can be said for all of these attempts to explain a fundamental human right. My goal is not to mediate this dispute, but to indicate that whatever view is adopted, similar action guides emerge. There is a common core to all of these accounts, and that core highlights the essential role and content of human rights.

Melden's fundamental right certainly involves significant freedom as well as basic well-being. We cannot pursue our interests if subsistence needs are denied or if freedom is drastically restricted. Vlastos's and Wasserstrom's rights to well-being and freedom can generate a right to equal treatment, for these theorists base their defense of rights on equal inherent worth of persons, as indicated by similarities among human beings. The resulting equal rights to well-being and freedom would imply equal treatment in the appropriate way. On the other hand, Richard's right to equal treatment can (as he describes it) easily generate a right to freedom, since he develops the right in terms of the capacity for autonomy. And respect for the autonomy of persons will have to include respect for the physical prerequisites for autonomy, or, in other words, well-being.

The reason for the overlap is that these views — and accounts of rights in general — are based on a common perception of what things human rights are intended to protect. Underlying each view is a conception of personhood, in the sense of moral agency. The connection between human rights and personhood is emphasized in terms of the range of application and the justification of rights. It is common to speak of human rights as applying to human beings because they are moral agents (perhaps extending to humans that are potential or past moral agents).

Melden's analysis of the central human right to pursue one's own interests is elaborated as "a right that [an individual] has as the moral agent that he is."[8] Personhood or moral agency is fundamental, and in some cases, Melden seems to interpret the basic right in terms of treatment as a person: anyone can "demand redress for the damage he has suffered in being subjected to treatment as if he were not a full-fledged moral agent, in respect of which anyone is on equal terms with anyone else and in this sense equally a member of the moral community of persons."[9] Richards generates the basic right to equal treatment out of a conception of moral agency. "The idea of human rights expresses a normative attitude of respect for the capacity of ordinary persons for rational autonomy."[10] It is not up to the servile person, who is happy to be pushed about by others, to treat others as he or she would like to be treated. What is fundamental to human rights is not simply that human beings treat each other equally but that each be given treatment at a certain level, as a person. It will follow that such beings, as full-fledged members of the moral community, will be treated equally in significant respects; but a right to equal treatment is based on an understanding of the proper treatment of persons.

What follows is that no matter how the fundamental human right is explicitly stated, similar action guides will result. It is not necessary to look at the diverse formulations of the content of human rights as competing alternatives. Since rights function as guides, any general account of the features of personhood in need of special protection will do the job. No matter which account one chooses, it will need significant development in difficult cases.

No matter how they are explicitly described, human rights provide limited but crucial protection for personhood. Whether or not one *enhances* the welfare of others, one must at least enable individuals to become and to maintain themselves as persons, as full members of the moral community. This protection corresponds to a moral minimum and provides a suitable dividing line between rights and other action guides. It is common to distinguish moral obligations or action guides in terms of (1) those demands that are morally required, and whose violation justifies punishment of some sort, and (2) those guides that represent goals or ideals to strive for and do not justify significant responses for failure to comply. The first type, those that are requirements, constitute the demands individuals must follow if they are to qualify as moral in even a minimal sense. The demands associated with rights occupy this category.

Many popular rights, like a right to life, to relief from physical pain, and to the pursuit of one's interests, can be explained as ways of treating individuals as persons. The elaboration of specific rights will proceed, however, within the limited scope of human rights. Rights will only require treatment necessary to enable individuals to become and to maintain themselves as persons. A right to freedom will yield a presumption against interference as far as is necessary to protect or to maintain the individual as a functioning agent, as a being that can and does chart the direction of his or her life. Such a limited interpretation of a right to freedom will leave room for a number of restrictions on individuals. Some paternalistic legislation, like that requiring seat belt use in automobiles, may be consistent with a right to freedom in these terms. Though these laws can interfere with a specific choice (not to wear seat belts), the minimal nature of the interference and the significant protection for personhood that can result may make the legislation appropriate.

In order to violate such rights, one must do something that (unjustifiably) involves *not* treating someone as a person. One can treat people rudely, meanly, or condescendingly but still recognize them as persons, as functioning moral agents. This is not to say that one ought to be mean or rude, but that such moral faults do not represent violations of rights. The special nature of rights and their crucial importance are based on the same point, that rights provide protection for what is necessary to develop and maintain individuals as persons. Once again, the demands of contemporary political movements illustrate the point. When Blacks, other minorities, and women demand that their human rights be respected and protected in law, they are concerned not about being treated rudely but about being denied such things as employment — and even education — in professional occupations. Rights movements have arisen in response to long-standing policies and attitudes that have resulted in certain members of our community being treated as less than persons, as 'second-class citizens.'

Indeed, Wasserstrom develops his philosophical account of human rights as a basis for criticizing attempts to deny Blacks treatment as persons. He puts the crucial fault of White supremacists in just those terms.[11] To deny rights to members of a specific race is to lead to a society that in blatant and subtle ways "forgets" that members of the particular racial group are full members of our moral community. Wasserstrom relates the case of a newspaper's report of a high-school band program. The paper emphasized that all high-school students in the city participated in the program. But Wasserstrom notes, "Negro children neither were nor could be participants in the program. The article, however, saw no need to point this out. I submit that it neglected to do so not because everyone knew the fact, but because in a real sense the writer and the newspaper do not regard Negro high school students as children — persons, human beings — at all."[12]

It is important to remember both the extent and the limits of the scope of rights. To treat individuals well involves more than respecting their rights. If the special nature of rights as the most important type of general moral obligation is to be maintained, the scope of rights must be limited. Emphasis on features necessary to treat human beings as persons can provide the necessary limitations while still generating sufficient content to make human rights informative.

A reliance on personhood brings out the essential reason for ascribing to human beings the special protection afforded by rights: the ability of human beings to control the direction of their lives in significant ways. This capacity led to the basic moral considerations of individual worth and freedom, and rights have often been associated with deontological theories, such as Kant's, which emphasize this consideration. But welfare considerations can also be uncovered here. Persons are also physical beings, and respect for the physical existence of persons is a prerequisite for the exercise of the ability to direct one's life.

4. The Role of Human Rights

Respecting personhood encompasses many things, from protecting physical life, to enabling intellectual capacities to develop, to respecting choices. These diverse obligations can at times conflict. The abortion debate is often described as a clash between the right to life and the right to choose. Euthanasia dilemmas often involve the same controversy, when individuals ask to be put to death rather than endure a painful, debilitating, and terminal illness any longer.

As long as specific rights like those to life and to choice are understood as elaborations of a fundamental respect for personhood, it is easy to see what in principle would count as relevant and sufficiently strong reasons for acting against an obligation associated with a right. As a general criterion, legitimate reasons would arise when respect for personhood in one sense is more important than respect for personhood in a conflicting sense. This explanation follows Gregory Vlastos's strategy of finding reasons for specific rejections of rights that are the same as the reasons for holding them in general.[13] Can one person's (e.g., an elected official's) right to privacy concerning how much he or she earns outweigh other people's (e.g., constituents') right to know where a public official's income comes from? When different rights support conflicting actions, one is forced to decide which sense of personhood is most pressing in the specific case.

This criterion helps to explain the special nature of rights, for it underscores the limits on ways rights can be overridden. The obligations associated with rights will not be justifiably overridden by other types of moral obligations that might be owed persons. For example, obligations of gratitude, of repaying a good deed, will not outweigh a right. It is clearly inappropriate to steal a watch (that is, to violate someone's property rights) in order to offer the watch as a thank you to a friend who helped you with a project. Since rights represent the strongest possible moral demands, the general obligations associated with rights outweigh other types and, thus, are almost always immediately translated into action.

Of course, it is still not clear in what circumstances one obligation of right should be acted on rather than another. The criterion developed above provides a way to approach difficult cases, but it does not generate a ranking of specific rights. Serious questions remain concerning how to act in specific cases. But to answer such questions, one must look to each particular situation (in terms of applications, at stage three), not to a theory of rights (as general obligations, at stage two).

Many people have, on the other hand, included these practical problems within the scope of a theory of rights. Some of the most difficult problems for many theories concern how to sort out and to weigh rights, that is, general criteria for when a right to liberty would outrank a right to life. Richards argues for the importance of achieving "the desideratum of a general theory of rights which explicates the complex ways in which rights are invoked and weighed."[14]

It is easy to see how issues about the ranking of rights have crept into many discussions. Theories that tie rights directly to action (stage three), not to general obligations (stage two), cannot fully separate the issue of what the right is from that of how to decide disputes. On such views, a right to life may come into direct conflict with a right to choose — as in the case of abortion. If a right to life is a direct demand for action and, therefore, means that others must not kill persons except in certain exceptional circumstances, then no one knows exactly what the right requires until all of the exceptional cases are detailed. Until then, the range of application and, thus, the force and content of each right will remain uncertain.

Unfortunately, there is often no quick answer to questions about which right is most important in specific cases. This is due partly to the fact that cases in which rights clash often represent some of the most difficult moral problems. In addition, the number of situations that represent clashes of rights is huge, making the task of detailing all possible exceptions to rights unmanageable.

It is no wonder that, after innumerable calls for rankings of rights, the goal seems no nearer. It may well be unattainable. If human rights are described in a manner that requires a ranking of the rights themselves, there may be no way to develop an adequate account of rights. At the least, it would be necessary to admit that we do not yet (and will not for quite some time) have a complete account. To admit this is to leave the content of rights uncertain and to make the use of rights in moral discussions problematic. Given other important functions rights perform, such uncertainty would be unfortunate.

Fortunately, it is not necessary to describe rights in a way that requires a ranking of various rights. The need for a ranking is a result of the failure to distinguish the proper point at which rights function in moral analysis. If rights are expected to function at the third stage, the level of specific applications and action, it is not clear that the rights in question are (what they demand) until conflicts are sorted out. Once it is recognized that rights operate at the second stage of moral analysis, the level of general obligations, it becomes unnecessary to decide conflicts in order to elaborate rights fully. As long as particular rights follow from the fundamental demand to respect personhood, their existence and nature are a unthreatened no matter what happens when different rights point toward inconsistent actions. As noted earlier, general obligations remain in force (and effective when no competition exists) regardless of how specific cases are decided at the applications stage of moral analysis. Clashes emerge at the level of specific actions, not at the level of general obligations.

As a result, examinations concerning what presumption of right must be acted on are not a matter of determining the relative strengths of the general rights. When rights support incompatible actions, a moral problem has emerged. One has moved to the third level of moral analysis and must evaluate and weigh the features specific to that case. It is not the relative strengths of the rights but a comparison of the features protected by the rights that will be decisive. Again, the ultimate question is what sense of personhood is most important *in the particular case.* Appeals to a (supposedly) stronger right will only delay the inevitable analysis of the specific features of the case.

The description of rights as expressing general obligations also points out the fundamental role of rights. These commodities serve to define a particular level of moral worth. Rights delineate respects in which persons, because of the type of being they are, deserve the highest moral status possible. This role is at the heart of early literature on rights. It is not an accident that rights theories arose as Europe was advancing out of a feudal system in which many human beings were treated as property and not as persons. Locke was ultimately concerned with guaranteeing that individuals be considered as beings who could control their lives and who were not subject to the whims of monarchs or religious authorities. Rousseau carried on the task, arguing also against economic oppression of human beings.

Such a goal in no way implies that a general theory of rights must always fully determine actions. There is very little discussion in the works of Locke or other early theorists on rights concerning how to decide cases in which different rights support conflicting actions. These issues were not relevant. The reason for invoking rights was to emphasize that all human beings should be brought into the moral community as full members. Conflicts can emerge only after the bearers of the rights are accorded the status of persons, with presumptions of a certain type of treatment.

Rights do enough if they establish a high level of moral worth for persons. The most grievous moral fault is to fail to provide beings with the status they deserve. Rights, given their history and their basis, are necessarily assigned the role of marking off and ascribing the appropriate moral standing for persons. A certain basic level of worth is owed each human being, not out of any bargain or preference, but as a matter of right. Considering the number of instances in which various human beings are not accorded the moral status they are owed, it remains essential that invoking one's rights represents simply, clearly, and cogently the demand to be treated as a person.

5. Postscript on the Range of Rights

The previous discussions have spoken loosely of *human* rights, and of the fundamental human right to treatment as a person. But not all humans are persons in the sense of beings who can deliberate, decide, and act on their own. Many human beings are not responsible agents, due to profound mental handicaps, old age, or youth. Do these individuals not get human rights? After all, infants and severely retarded human beings may resemble persons in fewer respects than do dogs or cats. If human rights are based on a conception of personhood, why should they be extended to humans that do not qualify as persons?

Before grappling with this problem, it is important to understand what is being asked. To say that rights ought to be extended to all human beings is to say that all human beings are legitimate bearers of rights. This need not imply that all human beings ought to receive exactly the same *specific* rights. Young children, for example, may not receive the same range of freedom of choice (i.e., right to freedom) as mature adults. We can legitimately restrict the actions of children in ways it would be illegitimate to restrict adults. This difference in treatment does not, in itself, imply that young children are not owed any rights.

A number of difficult cases arise concerning what human beings should gain rights. I will focus on two such cases: (1) those who are not yet but will be persons and (2) those who never have been and never will be persons. The ascription of rights to individuals in the second category is controversial. On the other hand, there are strong reasons for considering human beings who can be expected to achieve personhood as bearers of rights. Included in this group are infants and young children. As noted above, children may be restricted in significant ways, but it is necessary to remember that these restrictions are generally necessary to protect their lives and welfare, or, in other words, to protect other aspects of personhood.[15] Furthermore, the fact that the choices of children may be seriously restricted does not imply that the lives of children are any less valuable than those of adults. On the matter of the right to life, there is no distinction between young children and adults. One reason for ascribing such worth to children emerges from the fact that every person has stages of life in which he or she does not possess the capacities for moral agency.[16] It takes a great deal of growth and development before the necessary capacities emerge. Thus, a respect for persons is legitimately extended to respect for the being who was or will be a person even during periods of life when the capacities for personhood are not present. (This issue will be discussed in more detail in Chapter VII.)

There remains the problem of those human beings who never were and never will be a person (for example, the severely retarded). Why ought any human rights be extended to them? At first sight, there may appear to be no reason to extend rights to these humans, but the answer may not be so simple. A reasonable (though perhaps not conclusive) argument for including all human beings under the scope of rights can be developed.

The argument emerges from the attempt to draw a line between humans that qualify for rights and those that do not. Indeed, it is not just difficult but impossible to draw such a line. A variety of factors — from rationality, to communicative skills, to locomotive abilities, to an understanding of abstract concepts — are involved with moral agency. There is no obvious minimum level of such abilities that qualifies one as a moral agent. More importantly, if one examines human beings, one sees no clear dividing line between persons who possess the capacities at an adequate level and those who do not. Personhood is not like having two feet. Either one does or does not have two feet; the capacities associated with personhood exist in innumerable degrees and combinations.

Unfortunately, any line one might draw to separate persons from nonpersons will be sharp; either one qualifies or one does not. The very sharpness of any division, however, makes whatever line is chosen arbitrary. Given the infinitely varying capacities of human beings for rationality, communication, and locomotion, to draw a line at any point concerning which human beings have sufficient capacities to be considered persons in the moral sense is to make a neat division that does not exist in nature.

Thus, even if we agreed that some humans would clearly never attain personhood, to say that those beings do not deserve rights would force us to decide at what level of abilities humans should have rights. This is just what we cannot do in a nonarbitrary way. Any line to be drawn between those humans who qualify as persons and those who do not could just as easily have been drawn at a variety of other points, for example, with humans possessing slightly more or slightly less reasoning ability.

Since human rights should not be ascribed in an arbitrary manner, one might conclude that the only clear line between beings with rights and those without occurs at the species level. Humans are the type of being that can be accorded rights (based on personhood); other animals are not. Since it is impossible to distinguish in a justifiable way those human beings who qualify as persons from those who do not, rights ought to be extended to all human beings.

This conclusion may be strongest, however, when granting rights to human beings who will never be persons does not interfere with or threaten similar rights of human beings who are or will be persons. In these cases, there is no need to draw a line. Caring for the severely retarded need not, in our society, imply that any other human beings are to be treated as less than persons. In other situations, for example, when life-support systems must be rationed between an individual who can be expected to make a full recovery and one who is in a permanent, deep coma, we may be forced to make distinctions among human beings. This would imply that in certain cases, the lives of some human beings (that is, those who will never be persons) will be less valuable than the lives of others.

Of course, these examples raise issues in the application of rights to specific cases. Given the difficulties of distinguishing between persons and humans who will never be persons, there remain good reasons for saying that rights, as action guides, must be accorded all human beings. Thus, the lives of all human beings must be given the strongest possible consideration in deliberations. It remains possible, however, that as these guides are applied to specific situations, the lives of some human beings will have to be chosen over the lives of others. But these would be very extreme cases, and their unusual nature emphasizes how difficult it is to deny the protection afforded by rights of any human being.

Notes

1. See John Locke, *The Second Treatise on Government*.

2. For Bentham's criticisms of rights, see *Anarchical Fallacies*, in *The Works of Jeremy Bentham*, 6 Vols. (Edinburgh: William Tait Co., 1843).

3. The two most popular accounts of rights link them (1) to *claims* (see Joel Feinberg, "The Nature and Value of Rights," in *Rights, Justice, and the Bounds of Liberty* [Princeton, NJ: Princeton University Press, 1980], especially p. 149) or (2) to *entitlements* (see H.J. McCloskey, "Rights," *Philosophical Quarterly*, Vol. 15 [1965], p. 118f.) For a discussion of these accounts of rights, see my "The Nature of Rights," *Philosophy Research Archives*, Vol. XI (1985), pp. 431–39.

4. Richard Wasserstrom, "Rights, Human Rights, and Racial Discrimination," in *Human Rights*, ed. A.I. Melden (Belmont, CA: Wadsworth Publishing Co., 1970), p. 99. Such a view is echoed by many writers. Bertram Bandman, for example, notes, "rights are among the strongest grounds for other people's duties." ("Are There Human Rights?" *The Journal of Value Inquiry*, Vol. 12, no. 3 [Autumn 1978], p. 217.)

5. See Ronald Dworkin, *Taking Rights Seriously* (Cambridge, MA: Harvard University Press, 1978), and David A.J. Richards, "Rights and Autonomy," *Ethics*, Vol. 92 (October 1981), pp. 3–20.

6. See A.I. Meldon, *Rights and Persons* (Berkeley, CA: University of California Press, 1977), and J.L. Mackie, "Can There Be A Right-Based Moral Theory?" *Midwest Studies in Philosophy*, Vol. 3 (1978), pp. 350–59. Feinberg bases the qualification for having rights on interests. See "The Rights of Animals and Unborn Generations," in *Rights, Justice, and the Bounds of Liberty*.

7. See Wasserstrom; see also Gregory Vlastos, "Justice and Equality," in *Human Rights*, ed. A.I. Melden.

8. Melden, *Rights and Persons*, p. 167.

9. Melden, *Rights and Persons*, p. 194.

10. Richards, p. 9.

11. Wasserstrom, pp. 108–10.

12. Wasserstrom, p. 110.

13. See Vlastos, p. 83.

14. Richards, p. 20.

15. Differences in treatment among human beings relate to Vlastos's account of differences in treatment of persons in order to equalize benefits. The obligations associated with rights may require different actions to protect the life of a child as opposed to a mature adult just as (in Vlastos's example) rights may demand different actions to protect the life of a person hunted by Murder, Inc., as opposed to ordinary citizens. (See Vlastos, pp. 84–86.)

16. A.I. Melden develops this point in detail. See *Rights and Persons*, pp. 120–23.

Stage Three:

Sample Applications

Chapter VII

A Moral Problem: Abortion

A s the popular debate over abortion indicates, the issue centers on two rights. Since rights represent the strongest possible moral action guide, when different rights support conflicting actions, important as well as difficult problems arise. The abortion issue qualifies on both counts. Those opposed to abortion argue that the obligation owed the fetus, based on its right to life, is decisive. Those who think abortions should be permissible contend that the obligation owed the bearer, based on her right to choice, is crucial. In raising this issue, our discussions move to the third stage of moral analysis: the application of moral considerations and obligations to specific cases.

Two questions need to be distinguished: (1) What is the appropriate moral judgment concerning abortion? (2) Should social action (for example, laws and amendments) be undertaken banning abortions? The answer to the second question depends in large part on the answer to the first. If abortion is murder (that is, morally impermissible killing), then laws against it would be proper. It is the initial, moral judgment that is most vexing — and that will occupy much of this chapter.

Two preliminary points must be made. First, only "standard" cases of abortion — that is, those without special features like genetic defects in the fetus or pregnancies that are a threat to the woman's life — will be considered. Second, the discussion will be limited to the permissibility of abortion in the early stages of pregnancy, the first two trimesters. It is necessary to mark some such line because there are significant differences, especially concerning the viability of the fetus and the risks to the bearer, between abortions in the eighth or ninth months and those in the second or third months. The differences may well alter the relevant arguments. To be sure, my division is a somewhat arbitrary one, but issues concerning exactly where to draw the line can proceed only after it is clear that there is a need to make such a division. The first task, the subject of this investigation, is whether abortion is permissible even in the early stages.

1. Personhood and Life

Those arguing for the permissibility of abortion often try to eliminate the problem by denying that the moral dilemma exists. The crucial claim is that the fetus is not a being deserving of significant moral consideration; it has no right to life. Mary Anne Warren distinguishes two senses of the term 'human': a biological sense and a moral sense. In the biological sense, anything with the appropriate genetic code would count as human.[1] Thus, fetuses, senile persons, even bits of (human) hair would count as biologically human. In the moral sense, a human being would be someone who possessed the distinguishing characteristics and capacities of the species. Warren has in mind the capacities that Kant emphasized in describing moral agency: rationality, complex communicative skills, ability to direct one's activities, and a conception of oneself. Warren calls human beings in this sense persons.

Individuals who consider abortion permissible often contend that only actual persons ought to receive the strong consideration associated with rights. Since the fetus does not qualify as a person, it does not have rights. Since the bearer does have a right to choice, this right will outweigh any consideration owed the fetus. Thus, abortion is permissible.

This argument, however, ignores many important issues. Though there is not time here to consider all of these questions, it is possible to question the claim that the fetus does not deserve the protection accorded by rights. The discussions at the end of Chapter VI indicated that rights could legitimately be extended to any human life — even to those beings that are human only in the biological sense. Those points can now be applied to the case of the fetus. Consider the following examples: (1) A person falls asleep and, thus, (temporarily) does not exhibit the capacities associated with personhood. (2) A person lapses into a temporary coma after an accident, but normal functioning is expected to resume after a short period. Neither of these beings is currently a person; each, in his or her current state, lacks reasoning skills and the ability to direct his or her life. Clearly, such temporary interruptions of personhood should not mean a loss of rights, especially a right to life. This point is obvious, but it yields a crucial result. To have rights, one need not be in a state in which the capacities for personhood are actually present and can be exercised.

In the relevant sense, not *yet* being a person qualifies as a "temporary interruption" of personhood. The crucial reason a sleeping person retains rights is that he or she will once again be a person. Consider how different the situations are for (1) a being who was a person and who is in a permanent coma with no chance of regaining consciousness at any level, and (2) the person (described above) in the temporary coma. It is obviously wrong to hasten the death of the second being, but it may be appropriate to, for example, "pull the plug" on the first individual. At the least, there is a moral question in the first case — a question that numerous physicians and judges have decided in favor of terminating life support for persons with no hope of regaining consciousness. Even for beings who were persons, the key issue concerns future prospects, not past capacities.

The future prospects of a young child are the same as those of the being in a temporary coma. Given proper care, each will become a person. To respect persons requires that one respect their existence (for example, their lives) even while they are not — or are not yet — persons. This seems to be sufficient justification for protecting the lives of children in the same way the lives of actual persons are protected, that is, with a right to life.

How far back must one go in ascribing a right to life to human beings? Historically, various points have been suggested: birth, quickening, and conception. Birth and quickening, however, seem too arbitrary. Neither point represents a sharp dividing line in terms of the development of a being. An individual just before birth is no different, in terms of capacities, from one just after birth. The same can be said for quickening, especially since this simply measures maternal *perception* of movement.

More importantly, the fetus, at any stage of development, is no less a potential person than the infant or young child. If a key criterion for ascribing a right to life is the prospect for personhood, then any being with such potential ought to be protected by the right. To determine how far back we must go, the deciding factor is when the being becomes a living entity that, given appropriate nurturing, will become a person. Again, this is a complex issue, but there are good reasons to think that the relevant point is conception. Before conception, there is no being that can be expected, with proper care, to become a person. After conception, such a being exists. Given this situation, though the fetus may lack capacities necessary for the appreciation of many specific rights, its life qualifies as worthy of the level of consideration expressed by a right to life. The brief discussions here demonstrate the serious problems for the simple claim that only actual persons deserve such protection. The conflict in the debate over abortion reemerges. The clash of life versus choice will not disappear.

2. A Stronger Right

Those arguing against abortion also try to end the dispute quickly — once the fetus is accorded a right to life.[2] The strategy is to rely on the relative dominance of life compared to choice. Since life is a more important value than choice, the right to life is stronger than the right to choice. As a result, in a clash between these two rights, life wins. The fetus cannot justifiably be aborted.

Again, our earlier discussions, in Chapter VI, cast doubt on such an argument. Rights are not fruitfully weighed against each other in general terms. Each right, as an action guide, is as strong as any other. As guides, however, rights need to be applied to actions. When two rights support different actions, a moral problem arises. General appeals to a stronger right will not settle the issue; features of the specific case must be analyzed and weighed.

If any right could make a general claim to being stronger than others, the right to life would be a likely candidate. Even here, however, the claim to special strength can fail in many cases. To be sure, in many clashes between life and choice, it is more important to respect life. A person cannot legitimately choose to shoot neighbors (because a stereo is too loud). But there are other situations in which choice is a more weighty consideration. This is especially true, as we will see, when individuals must sacrifice a great deal to save a life. Individuals are not required to donate kidneys, even when a life is at stake. Such examples will reinforce the conclusion that it is inappropriate to use general rankings of rights in order to decide specific cases. It is the facts surrounding those cases that must be appealed to in determining what value is most important.

The abortion problem is too complex and difficult to be answered or eliminated easily. The strategies summarized above fail to recognize the complexity of the issue. Those arguing that abortion is permissible have contended that the fetus has no rights, so there is no real clash of values. Those arguing against abortion claim that the right to life, as a general action guide, is stronger than the right to choice. As we have seen, however, there is a clear clash of values here, and it can only be resolved by determining, based on the specifics of the abortion case, whether this is one of those situations in which choice can outweigh life.

3. The Conflicting Action Guides[3]

The first step is to elaborate the moral guides at the heart of the abortion debate. I will do this by detailing the demands associated with the rights to life and choice. Much has already been said about these values and guides. The following discussions are designed simply to raise the features relevant to the abortion debate. The first action guide, which favors those who believe abortion should be permissible, is that the choices of mature, rational beings ought to be respected. The significance of choice has been underscored from our very first discussions. An important capacity of human beings is the ability to make their own rational decisions; respect for this capacity provides the foundation for one of the two basic moral considerations. As discussions of the foundation for human rights suggested, the obligation to respect choice is most pressing when the decision in question concerns the very direction of one's life. A decision about abortion clearly qualifies. Powerful reasons will be required to justify interference with a person's decision about what happens to his or her body.

Respect for choice involves much more than avoiding force or threats in dealing with individuals. People — and society as a whole — have the ability to cajole, condition, or otherwise induce individuals to adopt certain goals, values, or beliefs. Such activity limits rational decision-making. Some indoctrination may be necessary and morally acceptable, but the fact that persons are generally sceptical of such interference indicates the strength of the presumption to respect human choice.

It is essential not to underestimate the scope of this guide. There are many cases in which choice can clearly outweigh life. People are not required to spend their savings or even a small portion of their income on life-saving medical treatment for strangers. To be sure, it would be extremely good of people to choose to make such sacrifices, but this simply reinforces the fact that such decisions are a matter of personal choice — even if a human life is at stake.

The second moral guide, to protect any biologically human life, obviously favors the antiabortion position.[4] The demands associated with this guide are broad; they militate against failing to care for those in need as well as directly taking the life of another. Humans who cannot maintain themselves, such as the profoundly handicapped and young children, are owed at least minimal care. There is also a further requirement (sometimes legally enforced) to render aid in life-threatening emergencies. To fail to provide such aid when it is reasonable and necessary makes one partially responsible for the death of the individual in need. Protecting life involves more than just not pulling the trigger.

This demand obviously applies when the life is a typical, rational individual, but it also carries significant weight for mere biological humans who are far from rational beings. If fertilized eggs and fetuses grew like crabgrass (but not as prolifically) in wilderness areas, it would be quite reasonable to say that people ought not simply hack them up. Of course, fetuses do not grow independently; others must bear them. Far from implying that the right to life does not apply to fetuses, this fact demonstrates that there is a conflict between the demand to protect life and the demand to respect choice.

The two rights alone do not, and are not expected to, solve the problem. They are not arguments about particular courses of action but statements of action guides which, given their status as rights, are fundamental to our morality. An understanding of the relevant guides does, however, raise the key issue. The obligation to protect life demands aid for those in need (for example, accident victims), but the obligation to respect choice allows individuals to refrain from giving aid when what is demanded seems excessive (for example, sacrificing all of one's savings to provide medical care to a stranger). The abortion issue will ultimately be decided in terms of whether what is demanded of the bearer is excessive.

4. Weighing Life versus Choice

The right to life is strongest when applied as a purely negative obligation, namely, do not shoot, stab, or run persons down with a car. Simply avoid performing actions that will lead to the death of any human being. Here, interference with individual choice can most easily be defended. Certainly, abortion is a matter of performing some action that results in the death of a human, but the issue is complicated by a crucial background condition. The reason for abortion is to relieve a burden that fetal life places on another human being. If that burden is sufficiently great to make it unfair to force a woman to bear it, then a doctor can justifiably eliminate the burden (abort the fetus), just as a person can, if necessary, kill someone if that is the only way to prevent him or her from intentionally taking the life of another.

The demand to protect life becomes less pressing as more and more is required to avoid killing. There is an inverse relationship between the burden that an individual must bear in order not to kill and the applicability of the presumption to protect human life. Parents who would bear great, long-term financial hardships to provide required but exotic medical care for their child are not expected to "go it alone." Community aid is often provided. There are limits to what is expected of individuals. When such limits are passed, the community may step in if it can.

There are many situations, however, in which the community cannot aid the individual who must bear the burden of supporting another life. Here, it often seems reasonable to allow the individual to decide whether to accept the burden. We generally do not consider individuals to be morally required to donate a kidney, even if refusal would mean the death of another.

In many respects, abortion cases are similar to organ donations. The possible medical problems and risks may be comparable. The chances are slim of contracting a disease that would be life-threatening if one had only a single kidney but not if two were available. Similarly, the chances that a normal pregnancy will yield (unforeseen) life-threatening complications are low. The physical risks from the surgery associated with kidney donations and the delivery that ends pregnancy are also relatively low. In both situations, however, the risk of death or serious illness is present. The existence of this threat is the major reason kidney donations are considered voluntary, not mandatory. It is difficult to require persons to accept even a low risk to something as important as life or physical health.

Further, the emotional and physical changes associated with pregnancy and organ donation are significant. Though one kidney is adequate for health, there can be significant psychological burdens associated with the recognition that one's margin for safety has been reduced. During pregnancy, a woman's body is no longer quite her own; it must be shared for a period. Actions and lifestyle must be altered. Even if the fetus will be put up for adoption, the physical and emotional strains of bearing it for nine months can be extreme. Indeed, the psychological trauma associated with unwanted pregnancies may well be more severe than those associated with voluntarily giving a kidney to save another life.

In both cases, however, there is nothing the community can do to shoulder these burdens. Organ donations will be necessary unless an artificial kidney is perfected. Until an artificial womb is invented, women must carry fetuses for the gestation period. The kidney donor and the person bearing the fetus must undertake significant sacrifices in order to keep another human alive, and these burdens bring the applicability of the moral demand not to kill into question. The choice of whether to carry the fetus to term is a very serious one. There are few decisions more important to an individual than those

concerning what happens to his or her body. The presumption to protect human life in its most pressing form (as a purely negative obligation) may be sufficient to justify interference with such choices, but
the burdens that make this choice so important also imply that more
than a purely negative obligation is at issue.

An understanding of the nature of the burdens also eliminates a
common objection to abortion, namely, that to allow abortion is to
allow infanticide, since there is no significant difference between a
fetus and a newborn. If the burdens associated with keeping the fetus
alive cannot be shared by the community and are too much to require
of any individual, it may be permissible to remove the fetus. Once an
infant is born, however, unacceptably high burdens need no longer be
imposed on an individual; the community can take on the burden if
the parents cannot or do not want to. Again, the key issue is how
much must be required of another person to keep the fetus (or any
human being) alive.

In comparing burdens, there is one significant difference between
pregnancy and organ donation.[5] The impermanence of pregnancy
raises issues about the extent of the burdens associated with it. It can
be argued that, with the possibility of putting the child up for adoption, the bearer is not required to make a life-long commitment to the
new being. Thus, given the importance of the value of human life, it
may seem legitimate to expect people to bear what are essentially
nine-month-long burdens of pregnancy. It is important, however, not
to minimize those burdens. Any risk to life, no matter how brief, is
significant. The inherent risks to health, the physical illness and
discomfort that accompany various stages of pregnancy, and the interruptions of life plans represent burdens that are not lightly imposed
on individuals. And, of course, the psychological and emotional scars
associated with an unwanted pregnancy and giving a child up for
adoption may extend well beyond nine months.

The ultimate question, obviously, is whether the burdens are sufficient to justify a judgment that abortion is, in general, a permissible
medical procedure. The analysis above indicates how balanced the
two sides are. The types of burdens in pregnancy are similar to organ
donation, even if the duration of some may be different. How significant is the difference between health risks that last nine months versus
those that continue for a lifetime? How much more serious are the

emotional burdens associated with unwanted pregnancy compared to those associated with facing the future with only one kidney? I suppose it can be argued that (1) actual health risks are more important than possible emotional burdens and (2) nine months of physical risk is significantly different from decades. But if these points were defended, would they prove conclusively that abortion is impermissible while kidney donation is voluntary?

I suggest that these distinctions are too fine to support a decision over such a significant question as the permissiblity of abortion. To make such a sharp, "yes or no" decision based on these small differences would be, in Aristotle's terms, to demand more precision than the subject is capable of. It may be necessary to admit that the sides are too well balanced to allow a conclusive general judgment about the morality of abortion. To put this another way, it is reasonable for people to disagree about the permissibility of abortion as a general medical procedure; there is no decisive factor on either side. The burdens seem to fall in a shadowy area between clearly minor (thus making the obligation to protect life decisive) and clearly major (thus upholding the obligation to respect choice).

The impossibility of a general judgment about abortion should not be shocking. Though we are inclined to believe that every problem has a definitive solution, the nature of moral disputes makes such a position untenable. In any clash of important moral values, there will be clear cases in which one value is more pressing, and clear cases in which the other is stronger. As we move along the continuum from cases obviously favoring life to cases obviously favoring choice, there will be a point at which the two sides are balanced. As the analysis here has shown, abortion seems to be one case that falls along the mid-point. The long and fierce public debate on the topic confirms this view.

It is important to remember, however, that the balance of arguments on abortion has emerged in the discussion of abortion as a general procedure. Though there may be no general judgment about the morality of this procedure, it does not follow that no moral conclusions about abortion can be drawn. Specific abortion cases must and will be decided, but they will be decided based on an examination of the burdens associated with each particular case. The burdens of pregnancy can vary greatly from case to case. Age, general health, psychological stability, maturity, and one's particular family and financial situation all affect the burdens on the bearer. It may, for example, be appropriate to make different judgments if pregnancy is being terminated to allow for a vacation trip to Europe or to relieve severe emotional and financial harms to the bearer. Indeed, the fact that the burdens vary so widely yields a further reason for avoiding a general judgment about abortion. Such a general judgment implies similarities among specific cases that simply may not exist.

Even at the third level of moral analysis, the application of action guides to specific cases, there are degrees of specificity. Moral obligations can be applied (1) to general types of situations (as we have tried to do for abortion) or (2) to very specific instances (that is, a particular person considering abortion). If a general judgment is possible, many particular cases will be decided quickly. If a general judgment is not possible, specific cases will have to be handled separately. The abortion issue represents one problem that requires separate analysis of specific cases — and that points out the complexity of applications of moral guides.

Many more points could be presented in the debate on abortion, but the general tendency will be to concentrate on peripheral issues. (One of these will be discussed in the next section.) The central question is whether the burdens imposed on women if abortions are deemed morally unacceptable are too much to demand. The analysis here has indicated that on the general level, the burdens fall on the mid-point between clearly too heavy and clearly light. It is for this reason that we are forced to examine the problem in more specific terms.

5. A Peripheral Issue: Responsibility

Those opposed to abortion often appeal to one factor that is presumed to represent a decisive difference between pregnancy and organ donation. The bearer is claimed to be responsible for the fetus while the organ donor bears no responsibility for the being with kidney disease. The bearer of the fetus undertook an unnecessary action, with the knowledge that pregnancy could result, that in fact led to pregnancy. But while it is clear that there is a causal connection between the sexual act and pregnancy, the issue of responsibility is not so easily settled. Leaving aside those situations in which the bearer (for example, young teens) are ignorant of the ramifications of intercourse, there are a number of ways for responsibility to be questioned.

We make a distinction between accidents and careless actions. The basis for the distinction depends in large part on how one's actions affect the risk of unwanted consequences. Consider the following cases:

1. I am having guests in for a spaghetti dinner. The sauce is made from home-canned tomatoes. In canning the tomatoes, I took proper care to ensure that the jars were well-sealed and were processed for the appropriate time. As can happen, however, something went wrong, the tomatoes were contaminated and poisonous. A number of guests die.

2. I am having guests in for a spaghetti dinner. The sauce is made from home-canned tomatoes. In the canning process, I did not take great care and simply guessed about how long the tomatoes should be processed. As can happen, the tomatoes were contaminated and poisonous. A number of guests die.

In the first case, the deaths were certainly caused by the sauce I prepared, but I would not be morally responsible for the deaths. I did not perform a morally unacceptable action; there was nothing more I could or should do to prevent the unwanted consequences. In properly preparing home-canned foods, the risks of unacceptable consequences are exceedingly low. As a result, it was reasonable to prepare and to serve the meal as I did. The deaths were, quite simply, accidents. In the second case, my actions made the risks associated with serving the tomatoes high. Since I did not process the tomatoes with adequate care, it was very possible, perhaps likely, that the tomatoes would become contaminated. Since there was much more I could have done to lower the risks so that serving the tomatoes would pose little danger to people, my carelessness made me responsible (and blameworthy) for the deaths.

To no one's surprise, two corresponding cases emerge concerning abortion.

1. Individuals (with knowledge of the possible consequences of intercourse) have sex while using birth control devices. The woman becomes pregnant.

2. Individuals (again with knowledge of the possible consequences of intercourse) have sex without using birth control devices. The woman becomes pregnant.

If people are to be responsible for the results of such actions, then the act must have been performed in such a way that the risks of unwanted consequences were high enough that people ought not to have performed the act or ought to have done so with more care. The risks associated with intercourse without birth control devices are high, but if one uses a device that is 98% effective, one has taken great care to eliminate the undesired consequences. If pregnancy results, it can be — and is — termed an accident. It seems quite appropriate that the moral responsibility of the bearer for the fetus be no more extensive than that ascribed in other accidents.[6]

It would seem to follow that if pregnancy results from intercourse when one was careless and did not take precautions, one is responsible and presumably must pay the price by bearing the fetus. But this point, combined with the conclusion that to take precautions is to avoid responsibility, yields an unfortunate result. If degree of responsibility is to decide the issue, the value to be accorded the fetus will depend on the nature and effectiveness of birth control devices used. If one fails to use birth control, the fetus must live; otherwise it can be aborted.

This conclusion seems unacceptable. It is similar to saying that one can, in defense of one's property, attack and perhaps even kill someone who enters one's land through a break in an elaborate security system, but one cannot attack and kill someone who enters one's property if a fence was not installed. We are inclined to say that the permissibility of killing a trespasser is independent of what one did to prevent people from entering. Once someone is on the property, one's responsibility for the person's presence (as indicated by the care taken on a security system) is inconclusive in deciding how to act with respect to that person. In the case of a trespasser, the issue centers on the reason the person is on the land. The judgment is much different depending on whether the person is there to steal or to get help for accident victims.

In short, responsibility for a situation may be crucial in deciding matters of blame and punishment, but it does not settle issues of current and future moral obligations. As a result, in terms of the strength of the obligation to maintain the fetus, the issue is not the extent to which one is responsible for the existence of the fetus. The fundamental question is that described earlier, that is, the extent of the burdens associated with the maintenance of life.

One might argue that if a woman performs an action with any chance that pregnancy will (directly) result, that person has an obligation to bear the fetus. The obligation exists no matter what the individual did or did not do to prevent the fetus from coming into existence. This claim raises the appropriate issues, for it moves away from questions about the responsibility for the fetus to questions about the universal obligations to a being such as the fetus. But what is the source of the obligation? It must rest on the value of human life and the resulting right to life. The original problem arises again. Should the right to life or the right to choice be acted on in this case? This leads to an analysis of the burdens associated with protecting life, and as noted in section 4, such an analysis does not yield a decisive, general conclusion. Discussions of the abortion issue will always return to the clash between the value of life and the value of choice. If there is no conclusive answer here, there is no general moral judgment concerning abortion.

6. Application to Social Policy Issues

Evidence concerning the facts about the fetus, the nature of the choice involved in abortion, and the degree of burden imposed on the bearer do not yield a definitive general moral judgment on abortion. In the social policy arena, however, decisions must be made. If action is to be taken, there are a variety of options, from gentle persuasion (through government studies or pronouncements), to educational indoctrination, to direct legal prohibitions. I will examine only the last option: Can laws or amendments proscribing abortion be justified?

Initially, it may seem plausible to side with those opposed to abortion and to demand that when in doubt, life must be protected. In short, the presumption to protect human life must be upheld in the law. With respect to the deliberations of individuals, such a position is quite strong. If I am not sure whether I ought to protect a certain life or whether I can make a choice to end it (perhaps in the case of deciding whether to cease medical treatment for a relative), I ought to protect the life. The same might be said for abortion; if a woman is uncertain about the permissibility of abortion in her case, she ought to bear the fetus.

There are some situations in which society ought, in questionable cases, to uphold human life; but these cases have a crucial similarity to the cases of individual decision-making described above. When an action in the name of society is at issue (as seems to be the case with capital punishment), society, like the individual, ought to respect life when the arguments do not clearly indicate that the life in question need not be protected. As above, the claim is that, when uncertain, the agent in question ought to act in ways to protect human life.

In such situations, however, there is no real clash between life and choice. The decision remains with the individual (or the community) that must act. But what society ought to do when acting as a whole and what an individual ought to do when acting on his or her own is very different from what society ought to demand (through law) that certain individuals do. While an undecided individual may be urged to hold off undergoing an abortion, more defense is needed for interference with the choices of those human beings who have good reasons for thinking that abortion might be permissible in their cases.

Given that laws proscribing abortion would represent general prohibitions, the problem is that there are not sufficient moral reasons for demanding that, in general, women must carry fetuses against their will. Because the values are balanced on this question, it is reasonable for persons to disagree on the need to protect the fetus. The obligation to protect human life has not been proven to apply here; this is just what remains in doubt. To demand or require that this obligation be upheld is to ignore the fact that the arguments are inconclusive on just this point. Thus, on the question of what a legislature should do when the arguments for and against a piece of legislation are equally weighty, the quick answer is that the legislature should do nothing. It should not pass the bill. As noted earlier, it is possible for specific cases to present sufficient grounds for abortion. It is in just these cases that individual freedom is most important. A legal system that seeks to respect the choices of its citizens will let them decide on their actions in difficult cases.

The emphasis on individual freedom at the social policy level emerges from an understanding of (1) the level at which the abortion issue can be decided and (2) the way the law functions. As emphasized earlier, the permissibility of abortion is not appropriately decided at a general level. Facts about particular cases must be investigated to determine the extent of burdens associated with a pregnancy. Legislation, however, is unable to handle problems that must be decided case by case. Laws operate at a general level; certain types of action are either demanded or proscribed. It is impossible in the wording of a statute to take account of the innumerable psychological, social, and medical factors that can sway particular abortion decisions. Since law, in essence, represents a general judgment and since no general judgment about abortion can be made, state action banning abortion is inappropriate. This conclusion will be elaborated in Chapter IX as an application of a general requirement for restrictive legislation, such as that proscribing abortions.

Notes

1. See Mary Anne Warren, "On the Moral and Legal Status of Abortion," *The Monist*, Vol. 57 (January 1973), pp. 43–61.

2. See, for example, Baruch Brody, "On the Humanity of the Foetus," in *Abortion: Pro and Con*, ed. Robert L. Perkins (Cambridge, MA: Schenkman Publishing Co., 1974); reprinted in *Contemporary Issues in Bioethics*, eds. Tom L. Beauchamp and LeRoy Walters (Belmont, CA: Wadsworth Publishing Co., 1978), pp. 229–240.

3. Material in sections 3, 4, and 6 was originally presented in my article, "The Legal versus the Moral on Abortion," *Journal of Social Philosophy*, Vol. XVII, no. 1 (Winter 1986), pp. 23–29.

4. Though I have stated the obligation in terms of respect for human life, I certainly do not wish to imply that only human life deserves respect. As the discussions of Chapter V explained, all life is worthy of moral consideration.

5. Some might argue that the question of responsibility also makes the organ donor case different from abortion. The kidney donor is in no way responsible for the plight of the person with kidney disease; the bearer shares

(at least in the cases I am discussing) some responsibility for the fetus. As I will argue in the next section, however, the legitimacy of abortion seems not to center on such issues.

6. This is the point Thomson makes with her people seed analogy. (See Judith Jarvis Thomson, "A Defense of Abortion," *Philosophy and Public Affairs*, Vol. 1, no. 1 [Fall 1971], p. 59.)

Chapter VIII

Whistle Blowing

I n recent years, the media have highlighted cases in which individuals reveal evidence of questionable practises by their employer. Such revelations are often called "whistle blowing." The media often portrays the whistle blower as a public benefactor who risks personal security and welfare to expose actions that are contrary to the public interest. The employer, on the other hand, often views the whistle blower as a disloyal agent who threatens the legitimate interests of the employer.

This sharp difference in reaction to a whistle blower is quite understandable. It is, after all, the employer who is harmed by the action, and the public interest (which media representatives claim to be serving) that is benefitted. The basic moral question is, when does one interest take precedence over the other? The issue is complicated because the employee has a special relationship to the employer. To highlight the issue, consider the following two cases:

1. A reporter is writing a story about a local factory. In the process of researching the story, the reporter discovers, quite accidentally, that the plant is dumping a pollutant that may in time threaten a major recreation area. Since there is no law restricting disposal of this particular pollutant, the reporter cannot urge legal action against the company. The reporter's discovery is news, however, and the story is printed.

2. An employee of a factory discovers that the company is dumping a pollutant that may in time threaten a major recreation area. On reporting this to management, the employee is told that such

dumping is not illegal and is not yet serious enough to warrant installation of pollution control devices. The employee then gives the information about the dumping to a local reporter for publication.

In the first case, there seems to be nothing wrong with a reporter printing a story that is uncovered quite legitimately — even if that story may bring pressure against the company to limit its pollution of the river. In the second case, it can be argued that the employee ought not to reveal publicly damaging information about his or her employer. The difference between these two cases concerns special obligations to the employer. The reporter has no special obligations to the company.[1] The employee, however, must be explicitly concerned about the interests of the employer.

The goal of this chapter is to uncover the competing obligations associated with whistle blowing cases and to provide some strategies for comparing them in specific cases. The point is not to judge individuals who do or do not blow the whistle, but to indicate ways to work through such dilemmas based on features of moral analysis developed in previous chapters.

There can be significant personal risks associated with such action. Whistle blowers often suffer serious consequences, up to and including firing. I will not deal with proposals for minimizing these risks. There have been calls for legal protection of whistle blowers and for mechanisms to encourage effective anonymous whistle blowing. A potential whistle blower may well seek such protection, but these considerations are issues only if the individual can determine that it is morally appropriate to blow the whistle. This chapter will examine that fundamental issue.

1. Whistle Blowing: A Definition

Many actions have been classified as whistle blowing. In this chapter, I will focus on a specific type of whistle blowing. Thus, I will adopt the following narrow definition of such actions. An individual engages in whistle blowing when he or she

1. is an employee,[2]

2. divulges information that he or she has gained on the job and that is known only by employees,

3. divulges the information to persons outside the employing agency,

4. divulges information about an action or policy of the employer or agent of the employer that can negatively affect persons or other beings worthy of moral consideration (for example, safety defects in products or in production processes), and

5. divulges the information in order to have the employer's policy or action corrected.

I will further assume that the individual has attempted to work within the employing firm or agency to have the policy or action changed. In other words, whistle blowing is not the first action taken upon discovering that the employer is responsible for an actual or potential harm.[3]

Many actions that have been called whistle blowing do not fall under this definition. For example, reporting to someone else within the firm on inappropriate action by one's supervisor would not qualify. My goal is to focus on the clearest, and perhaps most difficult, cases — that is, when an individual must debate whether to "go public" or not.

Finally, individuals have often blown the whistle even when there was no significant potential harm. Employees have, out of revenge for some real or perceived injustice, divulged information detrimental to the interests of the employer. I am concerned only with cases in which there are reasonable grounds for informing on an employer. Only here does the moral dilemma, the clash of competing obligations, emerge.

2. Obligations against Whistle Blowing

An employee has a specific role within the employing organization. That role carries with it special obligations.[4] Just as a parent must perform specific actions within a family, an employee must fulfill specific duties if the organization is to function smoothly and to achieve its goals. Often, the special obligations of employees are obvious; they are explicitly stated in the contract that employee and employer sign. The special obligations of employees that result from explicit agreements have moral force similar to that arising from promises. The parties involved, through their acceptance of the agreement, give themselves additional responsibilities.

It has been argued that employees have no other special obligations than those that they explicitly agree to. This position has been called the Contract Thesis. The Contract Thesis can be defended based on a defense of capitalism as a system that promotes freedom as well as general welfare.[5] It can be argued that a capitalist economic system can uphold these basic moral considerations only if the duties of employees are all and only those they have *freely* agreed to.[6]

There are, however, problems with this rather narrow view of employee responsibilities. From a purely practical point of view, such a position fails to capture the reality of many employment situations. Often, there is little in the way of explicit agreement between employer and employee. An individual is hired to work for a company in whatever position seems essential at the time.

When an employee fulfills a demand of an employer, one can say that the employee has accepted the order, but the situation generally has little of the bargaining associated with an agreement. The employee does not 'agree' to move from one position to the next as much as he or she 'obeys' an order from a supervisor to shift tasks. An employer's demand is generally not open for discussion, and the employee usually is in the position of following the order or facing some negative response from the employer. This introduces a coercive element into the relationship that makes the idea of agreement to the demands inappropriate.

No matter how much control an employer may try to give employees, there will always be limits to worker autonomy. The workplace exists to meet certain goals, and workers must perform their roles in the cooperative arrangement. Though workers may agree to enter the workplace, once within it, they can be subject to many demands that they did not originally agree to.

If it is reasonable for employers to expect obedience from employees, then workers will have obligations beyond those they explicitly agree to. We can speak of these additional duties as implicit obligations, that is, general obligations that arise given the nature of the employment situation. For our purposes, two such obligations will be noted: obedience and confidentiality. The importance of these implicit moral obligations is evident by the fact that they have received significant backing in the law. The *Restatement of Agency* cites these as two of the fundamental duties of agents — and employees can be considered agents of their employers.[7] Of course, the mere fact that these duties have been elaborated in the law does not prove that there are corresponding moral obligations. We must discover independent reasons for claiming that employees have special moral obligations of obedience and confidentiality to their employers.

The requirements of these two obligations are fairly obvious.

1. Obedience: to carry out the demands of the employer (or a supervisor designated by the employer) and

2. Confidentiality: not to divulge private infomation of the employer, that is, information received on the job and whose release would harm the employer.

To speak of obedience and confidentiality as obligations of employees is to categorize them as guides to action. It is important to remember that such guides do not yield absolute requirements. They function at the second stage of moral analysis and provide an account of some of the moral demands on individuals. Of course, as special moral obligations, confidentiality and obedience to employers apply only to those who have entered an employment arrangement.

In our society, the employee functions in a competitive economic arrangement that pits firms against each other in a battle for consumer dollars. Assuming this system can be morally acceptable, there are special duties that necessarily emerge for participants in the system. A firm can be successful only if it can expect certain behavior from its employees. For one thing, the firm can provide a good or service only if its employees are willing to perform the specific roles that are necessary for the production and distribution of the product. Since this is a cooperative process involving a number of individuals, there must be some hierarchy of authority, and those below must accept and work within the system coordinated by those above. Thus arises the obligation of individuals to follow the demands of the employer or designated supervisor.

Since a competitive economic system relies on separate firms operating independently, information about any particular firm must be carefully guarded. Temporary problems, knowledge about new products, and research failures and successes must be kept within the organization. If another firm were to learn such information, it could gain an unfair competitive edge. This would harm not only the original firm but the community as a whole, for there would be less incentive for any firm to undertake the research needed to generate new products or more efficient modes of production. Thus arises the obligation of confidentiality. In short, obedience and confidentiality are essential features of the employment situation. By agreeing to enter the role, individuals take on the special obligations associated with it.

We can now see how the special obligations of employees generate arguments against whistle blowing. The employee considering whistle blowing is not one whose role involves making decisions about the action or practise in question — otherwise the individual would simply change the practise. As a result, the employee most likely does not have all of the relevant information. Thus, the individual will not have been able to weigh carefully all of the factors involved in the decision. Further, the issues over which whistle blowing occurs often involve questions that generate significant and reasonable disagreement. To what extent does a corporation have obligations to the environment beyond those mandated by law? These are issues for those in executive roles to deal with. An individual employee may disagree with the corporations decision and may continue to urge that the decision be altered, but it is the employer's role and right to make the final determination for the firm. To blow the whistle is to take away this right and to harm the employer.

This conclusion can be extended to problems like product safety. A product that is clearly unsafe will be eliminated by market forces, without the need for an employee to blow the whistle. The only time whistle blowing will be an issue here will be in borderline cases. Take, for example, the Pinto case, in which engineers may have had evidence that the gas tank would rupture and cause a gas explosion in certain situations. Management may have argued, however, that this risk was not severe enough to justify blowing the whistle. No car will be perfectly safe, and management must make some compromises when weighing factors like safety, cost, appearance, and convenience. Again, management has the role and right to make these decisions. Individual employees can provide relevant information but must then accept the decisions of management.

3. Obligations Supporting Whistle-Blowing

The previous discussions have highlighted the obligations that employees have to their employers, but such obligations can sometimes conflict with other, universal obligations. With respect to whistle blowing, universal obligations concerning avoiding harms to people or other beings owed moral consideration can clash with the special obligations of obedience and confidentiality to employers.

The particular universal obligations at issue can vary with the nature of the problem that generates consideration of whistle blowing.

1. Threats to human life owing to defects in products: Obligations to protect human life imply avoidance of business tactics that can result in deaths or serious injuries to consumers.

2. Threats to property owing to inappropriate or defective products (for example, "energy-saving" devices that will cause heating units to break down): Various obligations, from avoiding deception in advertising to respect for the goods and well-being of persons can be relevant here.[8]

Numerous other examples could be cited, but there is likely to be an important common characteristic to these cases. The universal obligations at issue can be brought under the heading of a very general obligation to avoid or prevent harms. This obligation relates closely to one of the key features of whistle blowing: the desire to avoid negative effects on others. The central insight is that whistle blowing concerns action to ensure that individuals are not made worse off. This is very different from actively improving the lot of others, and the obligations associated with avoiding harm are generally among the most pressing.

The distinction between avoiding evil and doing good is often not sharp, but it does represent an important aspect of moral theory. Simon, Powers, and Gunnemann have distinguished between negative injunctions (such as the obligations associated with not harming) and affirmative duties (such as obligations to be kind and generous).[9] They argue that negative injunctions represent minimal moral requirements. Whether or not one is generous, one still must not kill. Whistle blowing becomes an issue not when one's employer fails to give to the United Way but when the employer produces and sells products that can cause serious injuries.

There is, however, a complication in applying the universal obligation to avoid harms to the case of whistle blowing. The individual blowing the whistle is, after all, not the individual doing or responsible for the harm. If the individual were ordered to perform actions that would cause such harms, it would be reasonable to refuse.[10] But perhaps there is a significant difference between performing the harmful act oneself and blowing the whistle on someone else.

The range of universal obligations to avoid or prevent harms can, however, be quite broad. The most obvious applications concern cases in which an individual may directly and intentionally perform an action that would cause harm to another. But consider the following example presented by Peter Singer:

> The path from the library at my university to the Humanities lecture theatre passes a shallow ornamental pond. Suppose that on my way to give a lecture I noticed that a small child has fallen in and is in danger of drowning. Would anyone deny that I ought to wade in and pull the child out?[11]

The obligation to avoid harms is still applicable simply because doing nothing would result in serious negative effects for the child. The key factor is the harm itself, not who is to blame.

Of course, there are many situations in which an individual cannot provide the necessary help alone; for example, bystanders may not have the necessary medical training to aid the victim of an automobile accident, or they may not have the needed weapons to ward off someone who is assaulting another person. Thus arises an important corollary to the obligation to avoid or prevent harms. If one cannot accomplish this oneself, it may be necessary to inform those who can. In the case of accident victims, a call for an ambulance may be appropriate; in the case of an assault, a call to the police may be necessary. In the case of actions of an employer who is causing harms, a call to the media or to government authorities may be the way to correct the problem. There are, then, obvious and well-grounded ways that the fundamental universal obligation to prevent or avoid harms can sanction the act of whistle blowing.

Further, it can be argued that fundamental obligations like avoiding harms are essential to social arrangements that allow individuals to organize into subgroups like businesses. Consider Socrates argument, in Plato's *Crito*, that his obligation to the state outweighed any other obligations, since it was the state that made all other roles and special obligations possible. For Socrates, the state was not simply the government of Athens, but the community as a whole. Socrates credited the state with providing him an education, an identity (as an Athenian), and a share in the cultural and material wealth, as well as legal protection. Socrates felt that his overriding obligations were those that maintained the social arrangements that allowed people to interact, to cooperate, and to seek personal as well as mutual goals. A fundamental aspect of these obligations would include the duty to avoid harms to other persons.

Given the importance of the universal obligations that are threatened by the employer's actions, the employee must retain the right to inform about the inappropriate activities. This is often expressed as a defense of whistle blowing based on the employee's right of free speech. The employer cannot demand that the employee give up the freedom to express his or her legitimate concerns.[12] In such cases, the right to free speech upholds two extremely important moral goals. First, the exercise of this right provides substantial protection for all individuals in the community. Wrong-doing by employers can be brought to light, and the very threat of an employee blowing the whistle may encourage employers to avoid the negative effects in the first place. Second, the right protects the employee's personal integrity. The worker will not be put in the position of simply accepting any morally questionable actions by the employer. Rather, the employee will be able to seek correction of what he or she believes to be serious improprieties. Those who support whistle blowing claim that this is a freedom that cannot be denied any person.

4. Strategies for Comparing the Competing Obligations

The previous sections have developed the obligations that support each side of the whistle blowing controversy. Each side can present persuasive points, but the fundamental tension still remains. The argument against whistle blowing has emphasized special obligations that individuals have as employees. The argument in favor of whistle blowing has developed certain universal obligations that each person has regardless of particular roles.

The discussion of whistle blowing reemphasizes an important feature of many moral controversies. The solution to this problem is not a matter of discovering the single obligation that applies here, in the sense that we seek the single correct answer to an arithmetic problem. There are many obligations (or action guides) that apply in questions about whistle blowing. The challenge is to determine which obligation is most forceful given the particular circumstances.[13] In this section, I will outline three issues to consider when weighing the competing obligations:

1. the relative importance of various organizations in an individual's life;

2. when it is reasonable to accept decisions of others in authority; and

3. the nature, extent, and probability of negative effects on the various parties.

The argument for whistle blowing emphasizes universal obligations as prerequisites for social arrangements that make subgroups, such as businesses, possible. This point is taken to imply the relative importance of the universal obligations over special obligations. The special obligations to employers can be especially strong, howver. The individual's relationship to his or her employer is not like being a member of a social club. The role of an employee encompasses much more of an individual's life. The time and energy spent on the job and the renumeration associated with employment make the employment role one of the most important in an individual's life. Indeed, individuals often define themselves in terms of their job. Thus, while the basic social organization yields prerequisites, the employer provides many actual benefits. This can yield an important sense of loyalty to the employer. As Solomon and Hanson explain, "the member [or employee] has an identity in part by *being* part of an organization, by sharing its interests, and by having special concern for its well-being."[14] The special obligations cannot automatically be discounted when they clash with universal obligations. We can see some ways to sort these obligations as we examine the second issue.

Individuals often accept the decisions of others. Children (generally) obey parents; drivers follow the directions of police officers directing traffic; college students finish the assignments given by faculty. Most demands of employers are routinely followed. Difficulties arise when an individual must accept a decision that he or she believes is wrong. Can someone be obligated to accept such a decision?

Consider a somewhat analogous situation: the case of civil disobedience. Many people have argued that even if one believes a law is immoral, one ought not to break the law. One must work through the legal system to get the law changed. For both whistle blowing and civil disobedience, the key question concerns what individuals may legitimately do to change the decision. Is it legitimate to go outside the system (for example, to break the law or to inform on an employer), or must one be content to follow whatever avenues are available within the system?

Henry Thoreau argues that it can be legitimate to disobey the law on moral grounds, and one of his arguments can be helpful for the analysis of whistle blowing. He distinguishes between issues of expediency and right. Thoreau contends that votes in popular elections and in legislatures will be based on expediency, the costs and benefits to those voting. He notes, "Practically speaking, the opponents to a reform in Massachusetts are . . . a hundred thousand merchants and farmers here, who are more interested in commerce and agriculture than they are in humanity."[15] As a result, the decisions of government can often be immoral, and no individual ought to follow laws that he or she thinks are wrong.

Thoreau justifies going outside the system because of the way decisions are made within the system. His criterion can be adapted to whistle blowing. Policy makers in businesses can make decisions on a variety of grounds. The legitimacy of whistle blowing can vary depending on whether those deciding within the business undertake a conscientious examination of the moral issues or ignore the moral issues and focus on other considerations — for example, self-interest. In the first case, the disagreement on the proper course may be a legitimate difference over a complex moral issue. If, for example, an automobile design clearly satisfies any reasonable safety criteria but there is disagreement within the firm over whether to make a costly design change that would improve safety well beyond the reasonable criteria, a decision not to make the change need not imply that the employer is violating a serious universal obligation. Here, there may be more reason to continue to work within the system to convince those in authority to change, rather than to go outside the system to force change.

If, on the other hand, those in authority have refused to deal with the moral issues, there may be greater need to go outside the organization. Just as lawmakers may only consider the expediency of legislation, business policy makers may only examine the effects of a decision on the company's financial situation. Such analyses may consider such things as harms to consumers only in terms of the cost to the company, not to those harmed. This type of analysis can lead to policy that justifies serious harms for others simply to promote the particular interests of the company. If this is the strategy employed by one's superiors and if they do adopt a policy that would condone serious harms to consumers, then whistle blowing may be the most efficient way to correct a serious violation of universal moral obligations.[16]

Underlying the question of when to accept the decisions of others is the issue of personal integrity. An analysis of how decisions are made by the employer will not be completely divorced from issues about the content of the decision itself. The employee, as a member of the organization is, at least indirectly, a party to the decisions and policies of the employer. There may be times when a policy violates such deeply held values that the employee cannot acquiesce in the policy and still maintain the central importance of the value threatened by the policy. A biologist who considers respect for the environment to be a fundamental precept may determine that he or she cannot stand by if the employer violates statutes concerning disposal of hazardous waste. At some point, the principles and values one considers central to one's life may override obligations to the employer and any personal risks that accompany whistle blowing. This will also be a point at which one cannot accept the decisions of superiors.

Throughout these discussions, a fundamental issue has been the negative effects that would occur given the existing policy or action by the employer. One way to judge the appropriateness of the decision-making process as well as the decision itself may be to analyze the presumed negative effects and to decide if they represent a serious violation of universal moral obligations, that is, something that no one who conscientiously examined the moral issues could condone.

It is essential, then, to determine what the negative effects are and whether they really would occur. There are many complex issues here, and I will list some central ones.

1. Is the negative effect actual or probable? Whistle blowing may be justified in either case, but the justification decreases as the probability decreases.

2. What is the nature of the negative effect and how serious is it? The need to blow the whistle will be greater if the negative effect involves a threat to life or health.

Sissela Bok captures these two requirements under the heading of "concrete risk." This is to be distinguished from a "vague foreboding."[17] Whistle blowing can yield serious harms for the employer. Threats to reputation and loss of sales may result. Such negative effects must be outweighed by clear harms that must be prevented. Such concerns yield a further issue:

3. How substantial and reliable is the employee's knowledge of the harm? As Gene James demands, "Verify and document your information."[18] Documented evidence is necessary both to determine whether there is a significant negative effect and to ensure that those who receive the information can effectively act on it.

There is a further reason to seek substantial evidence: to reduce whistle blowing based on bias. As noted previously, employer and employee may have reasonable differences over the extent of the business's obligations. The worker's efforts to document the problem will provide further grounds for determining whether the employer's transgression is serious enough for whistle blowing. Such research, combined with any knowledge of the basis for the employer's decision, can help to eliminate inappropriate whistle blowing.

5. Conclusion

Clearly, there are many issues that must be examined when an individual is contemplating whistle blowing. The special obligations to the employer are significant, but there can be cases in which universal obligations — especially those involving the pressing duties associated with the moral minimum — can be more pressing. Once again, the controversy emerges at the third stage of moral analysis, when one finds oneself in a specific situation in which various moral obligations conflict. There is no short cut to carefully uncovering the relevant obligations.

Whistle blowing also raises issues beyond the moral ones examined here. As I noted at the outset, whistle blowers often face serious reprisals from employers. These risks cannot be ignored, and they have sparked efforts to provide legal protection for whistle blowers. Those arguing for legal protection have presumed that whistle blowing can be a morally legitimate activity. This chapter has examined some of the issues individuals must consider in order to determine if whistle blowing is morally appropriate in a particular case.

Notes

1. Any duties to the company are indirect. There is an obligation not to tell lies about the company, but this is based on the role of the reporting profession, not on any special relationship with that firm.

2. I will focus on employees of private corporations, though many of the arguments to be presented below also apply to employees of other institutions.

3. There is disagreement over when it is reasonable to conclude this. DeGeorge urges that internal avenues be exhausted. (See Richard DeGeorge, *Business Ethics* [New York: Macmillan Co., 1982], pp. 161–62.) James, on the

other hand, argues that whistle blowing may be necessary before internal avenues are fully exhausted. (See Gene James, "In Defense of Whistle Blowing," in *Business Ethics*, eds. Hoffman and Moore [New York: McGraw-Hill, Inc., 1984], p. 254.)

4. For more information about special obligations, see Chapter III.

5. Such a defense of capitalism was presented in Chapter IV.

6. Baier presents but ultimately rejects such an argument. See Kurt Baier, "Duties to One's Employer," in *Just Business*, ed. Tom Regan, (New York: Random House, 1984), p. 82ff.

7. For a discussion of the *Restatement*, see Phillip Blumberg, "Corporate Responsibility and the Employee's Duty of Loyalty and Obedience," in *Ethical Theory and Business*, eds. Beauchamp and Bowie, (Englewood Cliffs, NJ: Prentice-Hall, Inc., 1983), pp. 132–138.

8. Whistle blowing can also emerge from threats to the environment that affect nonhumans. Obligations to other living things, based on their capacities for life, growth, and (in some cases) pleasure and pain yield a concern for the habitat of other livings beings. In the above discussions, I will deal primarily with obligations to humans.

9. See Simon, Powers, and Gunnemann, "The Responsibilities of Corporations and Their Owners," in *Ethical Theory and Business*, eds. Beauchamp and Bowie, pp. 86–93.

10. As Blumberg notes, even in the *Restatement of Agency*, one need not obey if the order concerns something illegal or immoral. See Blumberg, p. 133.

11. Peter Singer, "Rich and Poor," in *Ethical Theory and Business*, eds. Beauchamp and Bowie, p. 622.

12. DeGeorge reports a more detailed version of this claim. See *Business Ethics*, pp. 159–60.

13. The answer may not be neat and clean (as arithmetic answers are). In some cases there may be little difference in the strengths of the competing obligations. This balance of competing obligations was evident in the discussion of abortion, in Chapter VII.

14. Robert Solomon and Kristine Hanson, *Above the Bottom Line* (New York: Harcourt Brace Jovanovich, Inc., 1983), p. 333.

15. Henry Thoreau, "Civil Disobedience," in *Thoreau: Walden and Other Writings*, ed. Joseph Krutch (New York: Bantam Books, Inc., 1962), p. 89.

16. For a detailed examination of whistle blowing and civil disobedience, see Frederick Elliston, "Civil Disobedience and Whistle Blowing: A Comparative Appraisal of Two Forms of Dissent," *Journal of Business Ethics*, Vol. 1 (February 1982).

17. See Sissela Bok, "Whistle Blowing and Professional Responsibility," in *Ethical Theory and Business*, eds. Beauchamp and Bowie, p. 264.

18. Gene James, p. 256.

Chapter IX

Morality and Law: A Requirement for Restrictive Legislation

Legislation, of all types and from all levels of government, is a major part of our lives. There are few activities people perform that are not touched in some way by laws. Driving to town is governed by numerous traffic regulations; even walking to town can be affected, for example, by jaywalking ordinances. Many of these laws are uncontroversial, but this is certainly not true of all statutes. A substantial part of the abortion debate concerns whether laws should prohibit or regulate such procedures. Through the years, draft laws — including current registration statutes — have also sparked much controversy. Similar debates have raged on issues from zoning ordinances to environmental regulations.

When is legislation appropriate? The question is neither idle nor easy. Each society will make judgments concerning when social demands, as evident through law, will be made on its members. These decisions will provide insights into the fundamental values of the community. Is the state to identify and support any particular religion? Should — or to what extent — ought the law to regulate economic activities?

Obviously, the reasons for and against legislation will vary depending on the content of the bill. But there are general issues that emerge given the nature of the law-making process itself. One of these questions concerns how the arguments for and against pieces of legislation ought to be weighed. An obvious response is that they ought to be weighed in the same way other types of arguments are weighed. The situation with respect to restrictive legislation, however, is more complicated, and I will argue that the criterion or requirement for the passage of such legislation is stronger than the criterion for weighing conflicting arguments in general.[1]

Before proceeding, it is important to clarify the type of legislation to be discussed here. Restrictive legislation makes demands on individuals independently of their personal goals and interests. Laws that prohibit certain deeds (such as murder) as well as those requiring action (such as paying taxes by April 15) qualify. Legal requirements on business that are designed to protect the environment or to ensure safe working conditions incorporate restrictive demands. On the other hand, a number of laws are not restrictive, because they do not make demands on individuals unless people want to use the law for their own benefit.[2] Laws concerning wills fall into this category. This legislation generates procedures that must be followed if one wants a will to be legally enforced. Since no one is forced to make a will (or to do it according to the procedures outlined), the legislation is not restrictive. It is clear, however, that much legislation — and most controversial legislation — is restrictive. These include statutes limiting abortions, requiring registration for the draft, zoning land for restricted uses, requiring payment of taxes, and requiring drug testing for employees. It is important to understand when such statutes are properly passed.

1. Justification versus Requirements

When is restrictive legislation justified? This is an ambiguous question; it has a strong and a weak sense. In the weak sense, it can be interpreted as asking what the relevant reasons for legislation are. In the strong sense, it can be viewed as asking when reasons are strong enough to justify passage of legislation.

There are many plausible answers to the weak question. Relevant reasons for legislation include:

1. Avoiding harms to persons or beings considered deserving of legal protection — statutes against murder, theft, cruelty to animals, and libel are justified primarily in these terms.

2. Protecting the freedoms of individuals — the Bill of Rights, with its protection for freedom of religion and speech, and recent voting rights legislation represent attempts to place respect for individual freedom at the heart of our legal system.

3. Providing for stable and efficient interactions among persons — traffic rules as well as banking and securities regulations are designed, at least in part, to accomplish this goal.

4. Undertaking desirable social projects — funding (through taxes or bond issues) roads, coliseums, and fairs falls into his category.

Legislation is not necessarily adequately justified whenever at least one of the above reasons can be raised for it. It is not appropriate, for example, to pass laws to prevent *any* harm to people. It seems wrong to make pulling someone's hair a criminal offense. Problems such as the difficulty of enforcement and the availability of other measures to deal with hair-pullers provide strong reasons against laws outlawing this activity. Thus arises the second or strong question: When are the reasons for legislation strong enough to make restrictive legislation appropriate?

The second question operates at the level of requirements for legislation. It concerns the criteria to be used when determining if particular justifications (whatever they may be) are strong enough. Should public festivals be funded as long as a large number of people will enjoy them? When are the benefits here sufficient to justify the infringements that come with the taxation necessary to pay for the events? Since it is not enough just to be able to cite a justification based on a relevant reason, some criterion is necessary for determining what counts as adequate justification.

In developing an appropriate requirement, I will often speak of the relative strengths of arguments concerning legislation. This is determined not by popular opinion or by the strength of lobbying efforts but by a sincere evaluation of all relevant points (or justifications). Even if the real world does not always mirror the procedure outlined here, the requirement developed below can provide an

important method for evaluating, judicially and otherwise, the acceptability of restrictive laws. All of us, at some time, question the appropriateness of restrictions enforced by law. We need some general
criterion for determining how to weigh the competing arguments
concerning specific bills.

The following two plausible options can be proposed:

1. Balanced Requirement: If the relevant reasons for legislation (at
    least) evenly balance the relevant reasons against, then passage of
    the legislation is appropriate (though it may not be necessary). This
    is not only a plausible position, it may be the most popular view.
    It implies that if the arguments are evenly balanced, there is a
    choice concerning whether to pass legislation. This seems to be
    our ordinary method of weighing arguments. One should, of
    course, choose the side with the strongest points, but when
    reasons are balanced, the decision can go either way. I will,
    however, argue against this position in favor of the second plausi-
    ble requirement.

2. Strong Requirement: Reasons for legislation must be significantly
    better (must clearly outweigh) those against the legislation. This,
    I believe, is the most appropriate criterion — though, as stated here,
    there are questions concerning its application. For one thing, I will
    not discuss what counts as "significantly better." I suspect there is
    no general answer. The criterion may depend on facts about par-
    ticular cases (for example, there may be an inverse relationship bet-
    ween the extent of the restrictions posed by the legislation and
    how much stronger the arguments for it must be). Restrictions on
    where people can park their cars may require less significant
    justification than restrictions on what individuals can do with their
    land. In this chapter, I will argue simply that more than evenly
    balanced reasons ought to be required for legislation. Since this re-
    quirement demands that arguments for restrictive legislation be
    weighed differently from ordinary cases, some special feature of
    legislative deliberations must be uncovered to justify the
    difference.

2. Elaboration of the Dispute

It is generally accepted, even obvious, that restrictive legislation
requires a significant foundation. This common intuition is most
clearly elaborated in terms of the particular justifications for legisla-

tion. Relevant and pressing reasons must be present. John Stuart Mill elaborated this insight in its most extreme form.

> The sole end for which mankind are warranted, individually or collectively, in interfering with the liberty of action of any of their number is self-protection . . . [T]he only purpose for which power can be rightfully exercised over any member of a civilized community against his will, is to prevent harms to others.[3]

In essence, Mill severely restricts the type of *justification* that can be used in defending restrictive legislation.[4]

The intuition that restrictive legislation requires a significant foundation is much less clearly developed when the issue centers on weighing conflicting arguments; that is, when the question involves the *requirements* for restrictive legislation. Patrick Devlin, while arguing against Mill's extreme limitation on restrictive legislation, still notes, "Nothing should be punished by the law that does not lie beyond the limits of tolerance[5] — and tolerance is to be determined by what is necessary for the maintenance of the community. Devlin, like Mill, spends much time developing appropriate reasons for legislation, but he does not settle questions about the appropriate requirement for legislation. He states that "it becomes then a question of balance, the danger to society in one scale and the extent of the restriction in the other."[6] Unfortunately, it is not obvious what should be done when the scales actually do balance.

The same uncertainty can arise in the legal system itself. Courts seem in basic agreement that restrictive legislation requires a "compelling state interest." But whether "compelling" is to be interpreted as "stronger than opposing reasons" or simply "at least as good as the other side" is often unclear.[7] This uncertainty highlights the substantive differences between the two requirements. The cases on which the requirements disagree are likely to include some of the most vexing legal questions. Consider the Supreme Court's landmark abortion case, *Roe v. Wade*. As the discussions of Chapter VII indicated, the abortion issue presents rather balanced arguments on both the moral and the legal levels. If a strong requirement were used, the Court could have admitted the strengths of the two sides and cited that balance as a reason against restrictive legislation.

Unfortunately, the Court took a different path. In discussing the question of when life begins, it noted, "When those trained in the respective disciplines of medicine, philosophy, and theology are unable to arrive at any consensus, the judiciary, at this point in the development of man's knowledge, is not in a position to speculate as to the answer."[8] Finding no constitutional evidence for the protection of the unborn in the early stages of pregnancy, the Court seemed to discover no reason (not "no *compelling* reason") for abortion legislation.

To be sure, factors such as the safety of procedures and the viability of the fetus were discussed (and provided "compelling" reasons for regulating and restricting abortions in later stages.)[9] But where abortion was considered legally permissible, the argument was not that reasons were balanced (and, thus, insufficient justification for legislation was present) but that no good arguments could be given in favor of the legislation.

The Court, however, has not captured the basic conflict between life and choice that surrounds the abortion debate. Perhaps this is one reason the decision is often considered unsatisfying. In essence, the Court has forced the arguments to a decisive conclusion. This is what might be expected if a balanced requirement were employed. In a case where the competing arguments were equally weighty, the position ultimately held by the majority must be defended somehow — even if this means avoiding issues or problems (for example, the question of the value to be accorded the fetus).

As many individuals, legislators, and judges have vehemently argued, good reasons can be raised for legislation against abortion. On issues in which the arguments for each side are well-balanced, it is important to avoid the temptation to make either choice seem significantly better than the other. Either side can do this, and the result may be vacillation on important issues. This situation may be unavoidable if there are no special requirements on legislation — that is, if weighing arguments concerning legislation is similar to ordinary cases of weighing arguments. But this is just to raise the unexamined question of whether the strong requirement is an appropriate criterion for restrictive legislation.

3. Grounds for the Strong Requirement

To indicate the plausibility and the source of justification for a strong requirement on legislation, I will compare three situations in which reasons for and against a particular action can be balanced.

1. An *individual* is deciding how *he or she* should act. Consider an individual who is deciding whether he or she should continue smoking cigarets. The persons has understood the evidence indicating the detrimental effects of smoking on health but does get a great deal of enjoyment out of smoking. As a result, the person is unclear about whether the risks to health are weightier than the loss of pleasure.

2. A *community*, through its legislature, is deciding how *it* should act. Consider a community that is deciding whether to build a new park. (I assume no new taxing authority is necessary; the question is how to use available funds. The decision, then, is not a matter of passing restrictive legislation.) The legislature has considered other possible uses of the funds and the benefits to the community from a new recreational area. In this case, the arguments are well-balanced.

In these two situations, outsiders may be of assistance to the agent deciding the issue by providing information and advice. But it seems inappropriate for anyone other than the agent in question to actually make the decision. The individual ultimately must decide whether or not to smoke; the legislature must decide whether or not the park is to be built. In each case, though outsiders may disagree with the final decision, either choice would be acceptable. If the reasons for and against smoking are balanced, the individual can decide either way. If the reasons for and against building the park are balanced, the community (the legislature) can decide either way.

Such situations differ from a third case, which clearly represents a decision about restrictive legislation.

3. A *community*, again through its legislature, is considering restricting *individuals* from performing certain actions, and the arguments allowing the action are equally compelling when com-

pared to those supporting the restriction. This situation may occur with respect to abortion legislation or, perhaps, marijuana legislation.

In all three cases, even if the sides in the dispute are evenly balanced, a decision must be made. In the first two cases, however, the agent making the decision is the same agent whose actions are at issue — though, of course, there will be effects on others that must be considered. It seems quite appropriate, then, for the agent in question to decide which of a number of appropriate actions to perform. This insight, when applied to the third case, provides a source for a special requirement on restrictive legislation. In the third case, since the agent deciding the issue (the legislature) is not the agent whose actions are at issue (the individual), the legislature ought not to pass bills when the arguments for each side are well-balanced. This is just what is demanded by the strong requirement. If the arguments concerning the specific bills are even, then the requirement for restrictive legislation is not met. The legislation ought not to pass.

Here is the special feature of restrictive legislation that alters the way arguments ought to be weighed. Restrictive laws emerge when one set of individuals (lawmakers) generates limitations on the actions of others (and, perhaps, themselves as well). The dispute between the strong and balanced requirements centers on the question of government versus individual control on questionable cases of individual action. If individual freedom is valued, it will take more to justify imposing limits on the actions of others than it will to justify decisions about personal actions. I may, for a variety of reasons, decide not to smoke cigarets. Even if I believe all those reasons apply to others as well as myself (the health hazards are, presumably, universal), I may not be justified in preventing others from smoking (where such activity does not harm nonsmokers). Other individuals must also be allowed to decide whether the pleasures of smoking outweigh the health risks.

A legislature's position need be no different from mine on the question of preventing smoking. Though empowered to pass statutes for the community, the legislature will operate within significant limits as long as the community seeks to protect individual freedom. The legislature ought not totally to ban smoking any more than an individual should — though it may be reasonable for the legislature, based on a concern for the health of nonsmokers, to limit smoking in public places.

The fundamental justification for the strong requirement, then, is that it protects individual freedom. The strong requirement applies to any community that upholds or should uphold the individual's freedom to decide questionable cases. It becomes essential, then, to understand when and why communities ought to accept a strong emphasis on individual liberty. To be sure, any community will allow citizens freedom to some extent. It would be impossible for a social authority to determine every action of every member. Some choices, however, are more important than others; and communities vary widely on the extent to which they allow individuals to make important decisions.

All societies, including Western democracies, face criticism for imposing excessive restrictions on people. In time, the offending statutes may be modified or eliminated. An obvious instance of this concerns the repeal of the prohibition on the sale of alcohol in the United States. Why should a society like the United States not impose standards of behavior concerning issues such as alcohol consumption? This is a more specific version of the general question concerning why societies should promote individual freedom.

As our early examinations of relativism indicated, different environmental, technological, and cultural circumstances may lead to very different social arrangements and rules, with varying emphases on individual freedom. As explained in Chapter II, this does not imply that morality itself depends solely on whatever attitudes or feelings exist in a community. Rather, differing circumstances change the ways that welfare, freedom, and worth considerations are applied. Mill, in defending his strict criterion for legislation, notes that liberty is only appropriate for mature individuals and mature societies. More substantial controls may be necessary for young children and for subsistence communities.

Mill's point provides help in determining the degree to which a society ought to protect individual freedom. In a small society, with limited resources and minimal technology, the dominant value may be welfare considerations associated with mere physical survival. In such communities, it will be essential for individuals to perform their roles in the productive system of the community. People may have very little say in what their roles are. Often, jobs will be determined by social mores or family history.

It is also possible for people to choose to limit their freedom in significant ways. In a society organized around religious ideals, individuals may leave decisions on many issues to those who, through training or special insight, are considered authorities on religious doctrine. As long as members accept the authorities,[10] they will leave decisions on difficult cases to others. Here emerges a second situation in which individual liberty may be significantly less pressing than other values.

The differences between a society like ours as opposed to a subsistence society and a religious community highlight the circumstances in which interference in individual liberty ought to be minimized. Our community is large enough and has achieved sufficient economic and technological development so that subsistence is no longer a pressing issue for the society *as a whole*. There are enough people and enough incentives to ensure, without force or serious social pressure directed at any particular individual, that essential jobs are performed. Thus, it becomes much more reasonable to allow individuals to make personal decisions about life plans and activities. The result is that the justification for limitations on individual freedom dwindles.[11]

Not only is our society advanced technologically, it also encompasses a wide variety of religious sects and ethnic and cultural groups. This diversity implies that there is no common religious ideal that would provide the basis for the limitations on individual liberty that mark a religious community. Similar diversity extends to recreational choices, including alcohol consumption. For many cultures, the production and consumption of alcoholic beverages play a role. There are, of course, serious harms that can accompany excessive use, and the community will have legitimate interests here, as in the elimination of drunken driving. But just as there is no legitimate community-wide authority to decide matters of religion, there seems to be no authority to make a community-wide decision about whether individuals should drink alcoholic beverages.

In general, the justification for a social commitment to individual freedom increases as a society becomes more advanced and as diversity among communty members increases. In these situations, respect for personal liberty will not threaten the social structure and will allow for the development and application of different ways of life. Since our society and many others today qualify as both advanced and diverse, significant respect for individual liberty is required. One indication of the extent of society's respect for individual liberty is the type of standard used for the passage of restrictive legislation. A community that does respect individual liberty will allow its citizens to decide for themselves when there is a legitimate question about appropriate action, that is, when there are strong and well-balanced arguments on each side. In other words, such a community will apply the strong requirement for restrictive legislation.

4. Practical Arguments for the Strong Requirement

Any legal system, even an unpopular one, requires public support in some form. In general, the laws must be obeyed. People may not feel any obligation to do so, but most citizens must in fact conform. They must not be willing to risk punishment. A legal system will not have the resources necessary to capture and convict a significant percentage of the population. Of course, a legal system that gains obedience simply because it can make effective threats is far from ideal. In purely practical terms, such a system is inherently unstable. If the threats begin to look ineffective, the system is likely to collapse.[12]

What is desirable is a legal system that most people accept as proper and feel an obligation to obey. Here, commitment as well as threat generate obedience, and the system can expend less of the community's resources simply on maintaining order. Commitment to the legal system will, however, be based on the extent to which the system protects and upholds the fundamental values of the community and its members.

For communities that do value individual freedom, public perceptions of laws and the system may be negatively affected when a balanced requirement is used. The balanced requirement denies individuals freedom in just those cases in which it is most important, that is, when it is reasonable for individuals to decide either way. If the law forbids a reasonable action, the interference can be viewed as illegitimate — especially (but not exclusively) by those who would decide to perform the proscribed act.

People who find restrictions in questionable cases illegitimate will be inclined not only to resent and to protest the law but even to disobey it. Such a situation emerged with respect to laws prohibiting abortion (where illegal abortions were readily available) and continues to exist with respect to laws against marijuana possession (where, on some accounts, at least one-half of American teenagers have tried marijuana anyway). In these cases, the law is often viewed as out of touch, as an irritant, or as insignificant in individuals' deliberations about how to act.

If the arguments for and against the proscribed action are equally weighty, it is likely that many people will decide the act is inappropriate. Thus, for any such law passed only on a balanced requirement, a significant number of individuals will be disaffected. The problem multiplies as the number of questionable laws multiplies. Those who find that many laws restrict actions that they would reasonably wish to perform may well become disenchanted with the system as a whole. The problems associated with laws lacking clear justification are simply added to the unavoidable problems of people who wish to do things that are restricted by clearly justified legislation. If the legal system appears to be at odds with a basic social commitment to preserve individual freedom, the system will suffer.

Legal systems may survive such situations, but the effects will be felt not only in the number of offenders and in public support for the offenders but also in the fairness and effectiveness of enforcement procedures. If a significant number of people are willing to ignore a law, police and courts will be hard pressed to enforce the statute. When many people violate a law, prosecution and punishment can depend on factors irrelevant to the issue. The law can be invoked as a way to punish some people for other, unprovable crimes (for example, presumed drug dealers who are arrested for possession of marijuana); it can be used against those who are less able to avoid the law (for example, the poor, who could not afford to travel to places where abortions were legal); or the law can be used against those who are more subject to police surveillance (for example, minorities, who have often been suspect by authorities). It is quite likely, then, that questionable laws will apply to community members unequally. Some will be at greater risk than others.

Risks of capture and punishment for violations of law will never be perfectly equal, but the differences can reach clearly unacceptable levels. Lon Fuller speaks of degrees of legality, that is, degrees in the way a legal system accomplishes the basic goal of subjecting human conduct to rules. Legal systems may survive but be seriously weakened by threats to their effectiveness. One important factor here concerns the congruence between the law as it is stated and the administration of the law.[13] This connection — and, thus, the effectiveness of the legal system — can be threatened by questionable laws.

Consider the following rather extreme case: A community has two different laws, one making possession of marijuana a crime, the other making pushing marijuana a crime. Even when people are caught possessing marijuana, however, they are very seldom, if ever, charged simply for that offense. The reason for this lack of enforcement is that so many people find the statute inappropriate and violate it that it is useless for authorities to deal with the issue. The only time the statute against possession is applied is when officials suspect they are dealing with a pusher but lack evidence to charge the individual for that offense. Here, we have one way the administration of the law can differ substantially from the statement and goal of the statute itself. If the only reason the law against possessing marijuana is invoked is to punish people for other, unprovable crimes, then the enforcement of the law seems inherently unfair.[14] Only violators who fall into a special category distinct from the violation of that particular law will face any risk of capture and punishment.

The injustice of applying a possession statute only to presumed pushers goes to the heart of our legal system. In essence, these individuals would no longer be presumed innocent until proven guilty. An otherwise dormant law, on which conviction can easily be gained, would be applied to them because they were presumed to be guilty of more serious crimes. Yet this presumption would never be tested in court, since the actual charge would be different from the crime that led to defendants being charged. Keeping in force laws that few obey provides the system with a way to gain convictions against people whenever the officials believe that these people have committed a more serious offense. Again, in a society in which individual freedom is valued, a legal system that often worked in this way would threaten the moral ideals of the community and in all likelihood would lose popular support.

As noted above, the number of violators will be an important factor in determining when extraneous considerations can play too great a role in the use of a particular law. As the police and courts become overtaxed, special reasons will become more and more necessary for the authorities to act on the law. In so far as the number of violators is likely to increase as the law is more and more questionable, extraneous factors like poverty and the suspicion of other crimes may be present more and more often in the use of laws passed according to the balanced requirement. Acceptance of the strong requirement may well cut down on instances of inappropriate selective enforcement. It is in this way that fairness of enforcement can also be enhanced by the strong requirement.

Thus, a society that operates on a balanced requirement can undermine its legal system in a variety of ways. Individuals may find that a number of laws take important decisions out of their hands. Such people may be more than disenchanted; they may resent and ignore specific laws or even the legal system as a whole. Once again, however, the difficulties for a balanced requirement are likely to occur only in societies that emphasize individual freedom. Only in such communities would people expect to make decisions over questionable actions and, thus, be upset at a legislature's making the decision for them. Again, the strong requirement gains support in so far as it is consistent with a well-established moral ideal.

5. Conclusion

The discussions here have not exhausted the issues surrounding the strong requirement. One issue, at least, is obvious: in weighing the sides in debates on legislation, what is to count as a sufficiently strong argument in favor of passage? As I noted earlier, there may not be a single answer to this question; what counts may vary depending on the nature of the restrictions being debated and the goal of the legislation. Even if a hazy area remains, the strong requirement can still do its job. It implies, at the least, that when arguments for a bill are equally balanced, legislation is inappropriate. This in itself provides significant protection for individual freedom. Cases in which individual liberty is most important are just those with a balance of arguments, where it is reasonable for people to disagree. The strong requirement demands that individuals be allowed to decide in these cases, and this implies a significant respect for individual liberty.

This makes the strong requirement the appropriate standard for our community — and an important way to assess the workings of the legal system. Our philosophical and legal emphasis on individual freedom implies that in difficult cases individuals ought to be able to decide for themselves. Practical concerns of a legal system designed to protect personal liberty also point to a strong requirement for legislation. As Hart notes, in a "healthy" legal system, citizens will "often accept the rules as common standards of behavior and acknowledge an obligation to obey them."[15] Such acceptance is threatened if our legal system considers that the choice on questionable actions belongs to it, not to the individuals who must act.

Notes

1. I do not mean to imply that much current legislation is inappropriate. Some will be, but many statutes may satisfy even strict requirements for legislation.

2. These laws correspond to H.L.A. Hart's (private) secondary rules. See H.L.A. Hart, *The Concept of Law* (Oxford: Oxford University Press, Clarendon Law Series, 1961), Chap. 5.

3. John Stuart Mill, *On Liberty*, in *Essential Works of John Stuart Mill*, ed. Max Lerner (New York: Bantam Books, Bantam Matrix Edition, 1965), p. 263.

4. For critical discussions of Mill's classic essay, see Peter Radcliff, ed., *Limits of Liberty: Studies of Mill's On Liberty* (Belmont, CA: Wadsworth Publishing Co., Inc., 1966).

5. Patrick Devlin, *The Enforcement of Morals* (New York, Oxford University Press, 1965), pp. 16–17.

6. Devlin, pp. 17–18.

7. A major reason that the conflict between the strong requirement and the balanced requirement often goes unexamined is that the dispute covers a very small number of cases. The only real point of disagreement between these two requirements involves the relatively small number of situations in which the two sides are equally weighty.

8. *Roe v. Wade*, reprinted in *Today's Moral Problems*, 2nd ed., Richard Wasserstrom, ed. (New York: Macmillan and Co., 1979), p. 8.

9. See *Roe v. Wade.*, p. 10.

10. There is much controversy about what would qualify as voluntary in these cases. Do individuals who are raised from infancy in such communities voluntarily accept the ideal?

11. Even in large technological societies there are still some limitations on individual choice based on the indispensibility of individuals occupying certain roles. In many localities in the United States, for example, police and fire fighters are not allowed to strike. Here, the potential threats to the community are considered to outweigh the workers' rights to bargain through a strike.

12. The situation in South Africa can be described in these terms. The vast majority of people in that nation have no legitimate reason to recognize an obligation to the system; they are simply suppressed by it. It is only the threat of punishment that maintains order. As a result, any attack on that order must be dealt with swiftly and forcefully, in order to demonstrate that the legal threats remain effective. This may, however, only lead to continued confrontation.

13. See Lon Fuller, *The Morality of Law* (New Haven, CT: Yale University Press, 1969), especially Chapter 2.

14. Income tax laws have certainly been used to jail mob bosses who could not be convicted of more serious offenses. Though these cases do resemble instances of selective enforcement, it is important that tax laws were invoked against others as well.

15. H.L.A. Hart, p. 113.

Conclusion

T he goal throughout these discussions, even in the applications to abortion and whistle blowing, has been to provide strategies for thinking about moral problems. Solutions to difficult moral questions do not represent a body of knowledge to be taught. What must be understood is a reasonable process for examining the issues. Our society's commitment to tolerating different opinions helps to ensure that each of us will be able to undertake this analysis, but this same commitment has led to rather ineffective training about how to think about moral issues. We are not taught how to make moral decisions in the way we are taught how to add. After early training concerning certain basic rules or action guides, people are often left to their own devices.

This "hands off" approach has fostered some of the simplistic attitudes discussed earlier. It is common to hear that moral disagreements are just a matter of personal preference. I think abortion is permissible; you do not. We simply disagree; we shrug our shoulders and go on with our business. This is an easy way out of extremely difficult analyses. Despite the popularity of leaving moral disagreements as differences in tastes, few people are really willing to accept this position in all cases. As noted in Chapter II, we want to say that the hit-man who kills people for pay not only has a different morality but has wrong moral beliefs. Our apparent inconsistency here results largely from a lack of understanding about the nature of morality. It turns out that the ways to analyze moral difficulties are not so different from the methods employed by other disciplines.

There are disagreements among people in many realms. Often we do not think the final decision is just a matter of personal opinion. When two divergent scientific theories compete, scientists will disagree, but not based simply on personal preferences. We expect each side to have reasons for its position and to be able to defend the position based on generally accepted data and some commonly held principles.

There are also generally accepted and strongly defended foundations for moral positions, namely, the values and resulting obligations that mark the first two stages of moral analysis. Even on such a divisive issue as abortion, the two sides appeal to considerations of welfare and freedom — and each side can accept, as a relevant moral action guide, the obligations emphasized by the other. Opponents of abortion do not think that interfering with serious individual choices is always perfectly legitimate; they simply contend that in this situation the obligation to protect human life is more pressing. The disagreement over abortion, as over whistle blowing and other moral conflicts, concerns how to weigh competing moral guides. In short, we need to know more than what the guides are; we need to understand how to weigh and compare them.

Once moral foundations and action guides are clear, we can expect — just as in the sciences — that the competing sides in a moral debate will be able to defend their positions in light of appropriate considerations and principles. In the discussion of whistle blowing, we uncovered a number of issues, from the nature of the decision making process in the organization to the extent of the likely harms, that enter any decision about the appropriateness of informing on one's employer.

Of course, in the sciences, we expect that there is one correct answer to any debate and that, ultimately, one side will be proven correct. Whether this assumption is necessarily true can be debated, but it clearly helps define public perception of scientific activity. Since moral debates do not have this characteristic, we might again be led to conclude that in the end, moral disagreements are a matter of personal preference. But once more we are led back to the difference between the abortion case and the hired killer case. Surely, while we may accept the intractability of the disagreement on abortion, we do not accept moral disagreement over the permissibility of killing for hire.

What is needed is a way to distinguish between (1) when it is reasonable to recognize that people have different but still moral positions and (2) when we can rule out positions as clearly immoral. The problem with the hit-man is the refusal to consider the efficacy of the general considerations of human welfare and freedom. As noted in Chapter II, the fact that some individuals deny this need not threaten the importance of these considerations any more than the fact that some people believe the world is flat should shake our belief that the earth is a sphere. In each case, the individuals refuse to accept relevant and pressing evidence for the points they deny. As the hit-man case was developed, his decisions were based on concern for his own interests, without any consideration of the interests of others (for example, the victims). In cases of killing for pay, any reasonably unbiased analysis of the welfare and freedom considerations will reject such actions.

It is on issues such as these, where the weight of moral considerations clearly tends toward a single decision, that societies and individuals often make moral progress. If we look at the history of the United States, we can see a number of cases in which an objective analysis of our values and obligations has led to changes in social and individual attitudes. Much effort has been expended to convince (and, in some cases, to force) people to accept that the values that were clearly applied to White males should also apply to Blacks and women. Part of this progress is an analysis of the facts, for example, that women do have native intelligence on a par with men; but, of course, it is possible to recognize that women have the same capacities as men and still to refuse to treat them equally. Ultimately, change can occur only when people are no longer willing to accept the moral inconsistency of refusing to apply values of welfare and freedom to beings capable of appreciating and acting on these values. Again, there is a parallel with scientific progress. It took many years and much debate to convince people that the earth was indeed a sphere. Of course, gains made on equality among races and sexes has not been nearly as complete as those on the shape of the earth. But this only shows that efforts to eliminate practises and attitudes that inappropriately limit the range of moral considerations must continue.

The two sides in the debate over abortion, however, can each appeal to pressing moral considerations and values. The special burdens that the bearer of a fetus must endure can yield a serious clash of values. On the one hand, people ought to be able to make choices that can seriously affect their bodies and life prospects. But people also ought to protect human lives, even of those who are not yet fully mature, rational beings. The debate, then, emerges within the moral realm; there are good reasons to seek to uphold the central values underlying each argument. For many such dilemmas, there may be good moral reasons for each side.

In such cases, we may recognize that there is no single, clear or obvious moral answer. Even if one believes that supporters of the opposing position are wrong, they are wrong in the sense of having mistakenly ranked the well-grounded but competing values. Debate and rational argument are possible and useful here. Since the positions do accept similar foundations and guides, we can reasonably investigate which value is most important. When there is a common framework (either common basic values or common scientific data to be explained), there is a common basis from which discussion can proceed.

If the values are closely balanced, as I argued in the case of abortion, debate — even long debate — may not yield a consensus. This, too, is to be expected given the nature of the discussions. Moral analysis generally is not a matter of following a procedure to discover the single, correct answer to a problem. Rather, it is a matter of working out a hierarchy of compelling but sometimes competing values. And there may be many ways the hierarchy can be devised.

How individuals or societies develop a hierarchy will say much about who they are and what they stand for. Decisions about whether to blow the whistle can do this. To the extent that one tends to favor obligations to the organization, one may be a person who emphasizes performance of one's particular role and acceptance of authority. To the extent that one acts to protect those that might be harmed, one might be a person who identifies with the wider community and evaluates issues for oneself. Both types of individual can be valuable, and any healthy organization may seek a balance of each. Of course, a person might become one type or the other without really thinking about it, but such an approach will not help when serious dilemmas cannot be avoided. To work out these issues, people need to understand the underlying values and obligations that generate the conflict as well as strategies for making decisions about when one obligation outweighs another. The discussions here have been intended to clarify the process by which we deal with the moral dilemmas that shape our outlook on life.

Index